What People Are Saying About

Mature Flâneur in New Zealand

Tim's writing is a mix of joyous curiosity, historical knowledge, and deeply thoughtful evaluation of the world. This book will make you want to travel to New Zealand while also giving the feeling you've been to the most special places and met the most fascinating people. This is travel writing at its best — a spiritually satisfying walk through the natural and cultural world with a narrator you wish you could meet on a backroad because his insights would make your trip come alive.
Michelle Auerbach, author of *Feeding Each Other: Shaping Change in Food Systems through Relationship*

Our favorite flâneurs share their far-flung adventures in the even more distant land of New Zealand. We get the vicarious thrills of visiting glaciers, rainforests, penguin habitats, and a steampunk amusement park. This entertaining mix of inspiring scenery, nefarious history, and resilient indigenous culture makes for rewarding reading.
Marsha Scarbrough, author of *Honey in the River*

I loved flânering around Europe with the amiable and ever-perceptive Tim Ward. So now to get his words and images on the very different world of New Zealand is a special treat. It's nearly as good as going — which, as always, he makes me want to do immediately.
C.C. Humphreys, author of *Vlad* and *Someday I'll Find You*

T0343798

If you have been to, or ever wanted to go to New Zealand, buy this book! Tim Ward takes you through the North Island and South Island discovering the beautiful, the majestic, and the magical places that make this unique area of the world so enticing. You'll find unexpected encounters even in the more familiar places like Auckland, Wellington, and Queenstown, as well as fantastically surprising experiences like an encounter with a Māori Warrior and (spoiler alert) penguins! Fabulous read!

Lisa D. Foster, author of *Bag Lady: How I Started a Business for a Greener World and Changed the Way America Shops*

The latest literary work by the wandering Mature Flâneur takes the reader on an exhilarating journey through the breathtaking landscapes of New Zealand (Aotearoa). From the bustling streets of Auckland, to the towering peaks, cascading waterfalls and stunning vistas of serene Milford Sound, each chapter is a captivating adventure on its own. Let yourself be transported to the hidden gems of the North Island, from the fiery geysers of Rotorua to the majestic Tongariro Alpine Pass, before venturing to the South Island, including the golden beaches and striking granite cliffs of Abel Tasman National Park. Ward is a magnificent storyteller who transports you gently from one fascinating destination to another. *Slow Travel in the Land of the Kiwi* is not just another travel book — it's an invitation to experience the magic of New Zealand.

Bart W. Édes, author of *Learning From Tomorrow: Using Strategic Foresight to Prepare for the Next Big Disruption*

Tim takes us to another world most people only dream of. His narrative of New Zealand comes illustrated with more than 100 photographs and spiced up with the conversations between him and his beloved wife, Teresa.

Anne Bonfert, editor, *Globetrotters*, and author of *Mein Traum von Afrika beginnt in Ghana*

Tim Ward's latest travel book, *Mature Flâneur in New Zealand: Slow Travels in the Land of the Kiwi,* is a delight for travelers and armchair travelers alike. Whether you are contemplating a trip to New Zealand or happy to experience it from the comfort of your home, this is the New Zealand book for you.
Lawrence MacDonald, author of *Am I Too Old to Save the Planet? A Boomer's Guide to Climate Action*

Tim Ward has journeyed not only across the world experiencing all the sights, sounds and delights our physical senses absorb but he's also gone into the world contemplating the deep questions that humans have pondered since we began to wander away from our origins in Africa. Ward's travels in New Zealand like his others take him both on and off the beaten path. One of my favorite journeys in this book was his discovery of a place I had never heard of, the Catlins Coastal Forest. Serendipitously, Tim and Teresa are recommended this place by a person they randomly meet in a cafe who overheard their American accents. They navigate this trip by keeping the napkin of recommendations from the friendly stranger from the cafe and meander and explore this forgotten place (at least to us foreigners) for 1500 kilometers. Reading this book will bring fresh perspectives if you have travelled to New Zealand and if you haven't... yet, you will want to. Tim and Teresa are master flâneurs: read this book... and get out on and off the road!
Neil Richardson, author of *Preparing for a World Which Does Not Exist – Yet*

The Mature Flâneur strikes again! In this evocative account of his three months' travels with his wife, Teresa, through the north and south islands of New Zealand, we are right there alongside Tim staring at Mitre Peak in Milford Sound in awe, rooting for the revival of the kiwi and albatross populations, and praying he is right that the Māori are on a trajectory of "de-colonization." Not only is this book a great read, you come away feeling smarter about New Zealand — the place, its people, the fragility of its ecology, and the fragility of our planet.

Stephanie J. Miller, author of *Zero Waste Living, the 80/20 Way*

Mature Flâneur
in New Zealand

Slow Travels in the Land of the Kiwi

Mature Flâneur in New Zealand

Slow Travels in the Land of the Kiwi

Tim Ward

CHANGEMAKERS
BOOKS

London, UK
Washington, DC, USA

CollectiveInk

First published by Changemakers Books, 2025
Changemakers Books is an imprint of Collective Ink Ltd.,
Unit 11, Shepperton House, 89 Shepperton Road, London, N1 3DF
office@collectiveinkbooks.com
www.collectiveinkbooks.com
www.changemakers-books.com

For distributor details and how to order please visit the 'Ordering' section on our website.

Text copyright: Tim Ward 2024

ISBN: 978 1 80341 748 6
978 1 80341 764 6 (ebook)
Library of Congress Control Number: 2024931596

A CIP catalogue record for this book is available from the British Library.

Design: Lapiz Digital Services

UK: Printed and bound by CPI Group (UK) Ltd, Croydon, CR0 4YY
Printed in North America by CPI GPS partners

We operate a distinctive and ethical publishing philosophy in all areas of our business, from our global network of authors to production and worldwide distribution.

Contents

Previous Books by Tim Ward

Literary Travel:
*Mature Flâneur: Slow Travel through Portugal,
France, Italy and Norway*
ISBN: 978-1-80341-535-2

Zombies on Kilimanjaro: A Father-Son Journey above the Clouds
ISBN: 978-1-78099-339-3

Savage Breast: One Man's Search for the Goddess
ISBN: 978-1-90504-758-1

Arousing the Goddess
ISBN: 978-0-97263-573-8

The Great Dragon's Fleas
ISBN: 978-0-92105-186-2

What the Buddha Never Taught
ISBN: 978-1-78279-202-4

Non-fiction:
Pro Truth: A Practical Plan for Putting Truth Back into Politics
(with Gleb Tsipursky)
ISBN: 978-1-78904-399-0

Virtually Speaking: Communicating at a Distance
(with Teresa Erickson)
ISBN: 978-1-78904-673-1

The Master Communicator's Handbook
(with Teresa Erickson)
ISBN: 978-1-78535-153-2

Indestructible You: Building a Self That Can't Be Broken
(with Shai Tubali)
ISBN: 978-1-78279-940-5

The Author's Guide to Publishing and Marketing
(with John Hunt)
ISBN: 978-1-84694-166-5

Acknowledgments

Thanks to all my friends and family for reading my many blogposts throughout our New Zealand adventure. You are the ones I am writing for first and foremost, and your notes back to me helped me feel connected and close even while far away.

I've been so fortunate to write for *Globetrotters* travel publication on Medium.com, where my stories have found a home among a growing community of travelers, travel writers, and most important, travel readers. I've discovered many kindred spirits and great writers within this community. My thanks to *Globetrotters'* team of fearless, peerless editors for creating and nurturing this group: JoAnn Ryan (editor-in-chief), Jill Amatt, Adrienne Beaumont, Ann Bonfert, and Michele Maize.

Thanks to the production and editorial teams at Changemakers Books and Collective Ink, who put such care into each and every volume they produce. It's an honor to work with you as both a publisher and an author: Vicky Hartley, Frank Smecker, Steve Wagstaff, Mary Flatt, Nick Welch, Ben Blundell, and Mollie Barker.

A special thanks goes to Anne Bonfert, Eric Bunge, and Mel Mailler for each giving me permission to use one of their stunning photos in the color section, and to Teresa Erickson, who contributed many photos of her own, especially those of me looking foolish. Thanks also to Najla Kay who designed the map.

Finally, and most deeply, I want to thank Teresa Erickson: first, for traveling with me up and down New Zealand and around the world; second, for being the best spouse and partner I could ever dream of; third, for patiently correcting the many spelling and grammatical errors in these chapters, and offering much wise editorial advice. Gosh, I'm a lucky man.

For Teresa

NEW ZEALAND AOTEAROA

Introduction

This is the tale of our three-month trip around New Zealand. How can two people take 90 days to see a nation when the vast majority of visitors see the country in just a week or two? Well, Teresa (my beloved spouse) and I believe in slow travel: exploring the highways and the byways at a leisurely pace. We are fortunate to be at a time in our lives when we can make travel our priority.

Teresa and I are both in our sixties, on the cusp of retirement, and as we own our own small business, we are able to take extended breaks from work. The Covid pandemic served as a wake-up call for us: what were we waiting for? We decided to take a year off to travel and figure out what we wanted to do with the rest of our lives. Early on, we discovered the French term for someone who does the kind of wandering we most enjoyed: *flâneur*. A flâneur is one who wanders without a specific destination, absorbing the sights and sounds, losing oneself in one's surroundings, and through that process, finding oneself anew. For a year Teresa and I *flânered* through Europe, and from that adventure I wrote *Mature Flâneur: Slow Travels through Portugal, France, Italy and Norway*. When the year ended, we returned to the US and spent a few months contemplating what we would do next. What we decided was, we wanted to be flâneurs for a second year.

A rare work opportunity took us to Mongolia in June, and from there it was a quick jump south (well, a ten-hour flight) to the land we had so often dreamed of, but never found the time and means to visit: New Zealand.

Having come such a long distance, we could not bear to simply skim the surface. We wanted to dive deep into this remote yet enticing place, to flâner without a plan other than to see all that we could see, and to do so slowly, savoring each vista, each adventure.

There are of course many other ways to see New Zealand for longer than a few weeks: for those under 30, there are working holiday visas. For older adventurers, there are other temporary employment opportunities, depending on one's career. On a beach in the Southlands I met an Irish emergency-room doctor who worked for several months at a hospital in Tauranga and then set off to travel; another couple I know accepted a six-month gig teaching skydiving near Queenstown. Digital nomads also come to New Zealand. On a hike near Fox Glacier I met a young American software engineer with a year-long visitor's visa; he was on Zoom calls with his US home office every night from midnight to 8 a.m. He traveled around during the days, and slept every evening. It worked well for him.

It's my intention that this book will serve as a source of inspiration for all who are curious about New Zealand. I hope our stories and adventures fan the flames of your desire to visit this amazing country. Or simply join us vicariously, as we explore the many wonders of the land of the kiwi.

Part One

North Island

Chapter 1

Upside Down in Auckland

At last, here we are, upside down on the bottom of the world. New Zealand has been on our "bucket list" for decades, but my wife Teresa and I have never made it here, until now. It's mid-June and chilly, since it's midwinter in the southern hemisphere. It gets dark at 6 p.m., because this is the season with the shortest daylight. Everything is topsy-turvy. Yet at the same time everything seems so bizarrely *normal* here.

"Auckland looks like a better version of Portland," said my beloved, eloquently damning with faint praise. Teresa is Portuguese-American. She has big brown eyes and long, wavy chestnut hair; marrying her is the best thing I ever did.

We are staying near the refurbished downtown marina, an area of chi-chi restaurants, gleaming office towers, and condos. The boats at dock are big and extravagant, including a New Zealand yacht that once raced in the America's Cup. Walking around the city, everything appears disorientingly similar to where we recently lived in the US, right down to the brand-name stores: H&M, North Face, HSBC, Citibank. There's a Starbucks across the street from our Air B&B apartment and a McDonald's down the block. The iconic Sky Tower looks a lot like the Seattle Space Needle, or to my Canadian eyes, Toronto's CN Tower. Auckland doesn't even feel *British* (apart from driving on the wrong side of the road). Everything's too new; it's not rundown enough to look like the UK.

Did we travel halfway around the world to visit a place just like home?

Only when we took the elevator up to the top of the Sky Tower did I begin to get an inkling of the ways in which this upside-down land is *not* like home. From the 60th floor of the tower one gets a panoramic view of the city, the port, and the surrounding islands. What is most immediately noticeable are the funny cone-shaped green hills that pop up here and there. These grassy hills are in fact extinct volcanoes. Geologically, this area is known as the "Auckland Volcano Field." It was a region of intense volcanic activity in ages past, with some 50 cones in all.

Auckland's Sky Tower

From the Auckland Museum, I learned that much of New Zealand is in fact *new-from-the-sea* land. Twenty-three million years ago this land mass was mostly underwater. Tectonic plates colliding in the Tasman Sea pushed mountains upward on the South Isles and rent the Earth's mantle further north, so that great gobs of subterranean magma spat through to the surface, creating volcanoes. The most recent eruption near Auckland happened a scant 600 years ago, forming the new island of

Rangitoto, just off the coast of the city. It rises beyond Auckland harbor, gray and sullen, like a mini-Mordor, a reminder of this land's unsettled recent past.

Auckland as seen from the nearby lava fields of Rangitoto Island

New Zealand's recent birth from the sea, isolated from other lands, put it on a unique evolutionary track. While plant seeds, insects, and birds could migrate here by air or water, there were no mammals — not even from Australia. No kangaroos, no koalas, no dingoes. Kiwis and other flightless New Zealand birds arrived with wings some 50 million years ago, then evolved to be flightless in a land free from predators (except eagles and hawks). That is, until humans arrived and brought their companion animals with them, both domesticated and pests (dogs, cats, rats, possums, and stoats). These hunters have ravaged native bird life.

New Zealand is relatively new to people, too. In fact, it was the last significant land mass on the planet to be inhabited (not counting Antarctica). People first arrived by sea canoe from East Polynesia scarcely 800 years ago. Their relative isolation in this faraway land led to the rapid evolution of distinctive Māori cultures.

I knew next to nothing about the Māori people when I arrived, and my introduction was at the Auckland Museum. It features exquisite examples of Māori art and craftsmanship: long canoes that could fit 50 or more people; weapons; ornately decorated hardwood communal halls. The Māori had no metallurgy before the arrival of the first Europeans: no iron, no steel. Everything was made of wood or stone or bone. The ornately carved ancestor statues and divinities clearly mimicked the facial tattooing the Māori people are perhaps best known for. The eyes were made of little black discs, surrounded by mother of pearl, which made the whites startlingly realistic. These statues have a presence of their own, at once regal and formal, and at the same time, powerful and fierce. I remembered from a movie I saw long ago, *Once Were Warriors*, that when the Europeans first encountered the Māori, they were warrior societies.

Left: Māori ancestor statue from the Auckland Museum. Right: Māori performer with *mōko* face tattoos in Rotorua

One peculiar feature at the museum is the number of statues that seem to be holding a ukulele in one hand — were the Māori some kind of minstrel-music-worshiping society? Well, clearly this is the problem with having too few data points. I soon noticed the glass display cases held dozens of different versions of these strange instruments. Carved of hardwood, whalebone, or stone, these were implements for war-making, not music-making. They were called *kotiate*, used like double-headed axes in hand-to-hand combat. Every statue of a high-status male includes one of these choppers, which was clearly the mark of a superior male's warrior status and lethal power.

I was transfixed by the Māori ancestor statues from the museum, and their *kotiate*.

The museum also tells the tale of how each Māori *iwi* (tribe) traces its ancestry back to one of seven canoes that according to tradition made the voyage from the islands of East Polynesia to Aotearoa, "Land of the Long White Cloud," which is the Māori name for New Zealand. Today, some 200 years after the first Europeans settled here, the Māori make up only 17% of New Zealand's population, well above the indigenous populations of the US (2%), Canada (5%), and Australia (3%). But, unlike these other Anglo-dominant nations, in New Zealand there's a vision of a land shared by two peoples.

This is more than simple reparations for past injustices and theft of land (although that is a big part of it). The Auckland Museum tells the story of the signing of the Treaty of Waitangi in 1840 between more than 500 Māori chiefs and the British

Crown. This document served as the legal foundation for the new nation. The museum also grimly describes the many violations of the treaty subsequently committed by British New Zealanders — including full-scale wars — and the long journey towards justice begun only in the past 50 years, when a commission was set up to address and provide redress for violations of that treaty.

Yes, there's a long way to go. But there's a principle at work that is truly profound: where the treaty has been violated, there's a legal and moral obligation for the dominant culture to correct it. At first brush, this seems fundamentally different from what I know of other colonizer-nations, like my native home, Canada, and my adopted country, the United States (to add to that: in 2023 Australians decisively voted *no* on a referendum on whether to officially recognize Aboriginals as the indigenous people of their nation). To be honest, when Teresa and I imagined visiting New Zealand, it never occurred to us how much we had to learn about the island's history of injustice and its progress towards 'de-colonization.' The Auckland Museum was an eye-opener for me. I realized that our trip would be more than a sightseeing journey; it would also, perhaps, be a discovery of a new, hopeful vision for the Land of the Long White Cloud.

After a week in Auckland to get our bearings, Teresa and I planned to explore the entire country, from top to bottom, for a total of 90 days. It was fortunate that we arrived in midwinter and not in the summer months when near to a million tourists race through the nation. From December to March, one pretty much has to book everything well in advance. You risk not getting to see sights that require a ticket, and not finding a place to stay in the busier towns along the main tourist routes. Yes, in winter the weather is colder. But it's not a harsh New England cold. Not Canada cold. When we arrived in Auckland, it was like a brisk fall day in my native land, and when the sun came out it was warm enough to venture out in just a light sweater.

Before leaving the city, we arranged to rent a spiffy white Polestar 2 electric vehicle for three months, in order to reduce our carbon footprint. The previous summer we drove up and down Norway in a Polestar 2, and loved it, despite having to learn how to master a whole new automotive technology — cables and charging stations and 'range anxiety.' Sure, there was a learning curve, but we managed without calamity. New Zealand's EV infrastructure is more rudimentary than Norway's, but there was enough of a network to make us feel confident we would be okay. As we headed towards the South Pole, under southern stars, the Polestar 2 seemed a fitting choice.

We vaguely planned to meander in a hazy, lazy figure eight from the subtropical tip of the North Island to the chilly bottom of the South Island and back north again. Our only goal was to see as much of the country as we possibly could, without ever rushing, just following our noses and taking our time.

Chapter 2
Rangitoto Island: After the Eruption

I was walking along the volcano when I thought I heard R2D2 in the trees. It was a weird combination of clicks and musical whistles that sounded as if they came from the plucky little *Star Wars* robot. I looked around and spied a medium-sized, black-and-brown bird winging between the branches. It had this strange little white tuft on its throat, the sort of thing a French aristocrat might have worn in a bygone age. When it settled, I was able to take a picture. Later, I identified it as a *tūi* bird.

Although to me the bird looked rather drab, save for its neck tuft, online I later discovered the bird's true colors: when the light hits those brown-and-black feathers just right, they shimmer with iridescent hues of turquoise, bronze, and cerulean blue. In ages past, tūi feathers were used to adorn the traditional cloaks of Māori chiefs. The tūi's calls are also colorful, producing flute-like whistles interspersed with coughs, grunts, clicks, and wheezes. These birds are mimics, able to play back everything from farm machinery to human voices. And they played a crucial role in the evolution of life on Rangitoto — New Zealand's newest volcano (see the color section, page C5).

Rangitoto erupted in Auckland harbor about 600 years ago, within the collective memory of the Māori tribes who lived nearby, and who gave the island its name. It means "Red Sky." At that time, a torrent of magma broke through the Earth's mantle — worn thin beneath New Zealand, where tectonic plates are still colliding. When the hot lava cracked the ocean floor, the seawater turned to steam, creating massive explosions that indeed would have turned the night sky red. As the lava kept coming, eventually it built a cone above the surface of the water, allowing the hot magma to spew into the sky. Lumps hardened in midair into weird, artistic shapes, before crashing into the rivers of lava flowing across the newly emerged land. As the lava flowed, the surface cooled and solidified, then crumpled when the lava rivers swelled again. This created vast fields of broken rock.

I imagined this raw, steaming land was much like all of New Zealand as it emerged from the sea 23 million years ago: lifeless, bare rock. In some ways, the story of Rangitoto is the story of New Zealand, but in fast motion. For the island today is mostly covered in vegetation and teeming with life. A trip to Rangitoto is a journey through lush forests and evolutionary quirks that are still puzzling the scientists who study it.

I took the ferry from downtown Auckland that arrives three times a day at Rangitoto and disgorges day-trippers (plus a few hardy overnight campers) at the single dock. It is guarded by Māori ancestor spirits carved on a wooden gate.

Māori carved gate at the dock of Rangitoto Island

There is no water on the island and no food. Visitors must carry in whatever they need, and carry out out all trash. Fortunately, there's a well-made trail from the ferry terminal to the crater rim, with a rough track that cuts across the island to a lighthouse on the westernmost point, and then along the southern coast. Most visitors do the hour-long trek to the peak, then straight back to the boat. But I opted (like any decent flâneur) for the circuitous route via the lighthouse, to avoid retracing my steps.

One of the first things one notices on the path is that there are big patches of raw lava rock interspersed with larger patches of vegetation. Helpful placards along the way explain how these islands of vegetation developed. The first arrivals on Rangitoto were spores of lichen and mosses, which gradually covered the bare rock. When they built up a sufficient layer of organic matter, seeds that had drifted over from the mainland took root; here and there, ferns and bushes began to appear, and then a few trees. With the trees came the bugs and birds (like the tūi) that feast on ripening fruit; the birds left their droppings behind, including whatever seeds they carried in their poop. And so wherever one tree emerged, a mini-ecosystem evolved around it. Little islands of vegetation gradually spread out across the lava field and merged with others, until today most of the island is a connected forest (see page C1).

The path to the top of Rangitoto allows for a detour to visit some of the tunnels left behind by the cooling lava flows. These proved to be cramped, dark, and deep. Rather than risk bashing my head on the nubbly, dark tunnel roof, or breaking my poor old knees with a long crouch-and-crawl approach, I opted for the shortest tunnel. I could spy a dot of light shining through from the other end. This still required feeling my way through, hands on dank, moss-covered walls. I had to squeeze through narrow, irregular spaces, contorting my body to match the shape of the lava tube, so that it felt like playing Twister while spelunking. Note to anyone considering this trek: bring a headlamp rather than relying on your smartphone light. A lava tunnel is not a good place to drop your phone.

A steaming lava field, with Rangitoto crater in the background

Back on the main track, as I neared the cone of the volcano, the path steepened and the vegetation deepened. The soil here was thick enough to support large, tall trees, so the forest more resembled a tropical jungle. Supposedly, in the nooks and crannies of these trees over 50 different species of orchids flourish.

Eventually I reached the rim of the volcano, some 200 meters (600 feet) across. A placard on the rim explained that less than 175 years ago, this cone and its crater were mostly bare rock — as evidenced by a reproduction of a sketch by an artist from the mid-nineteenth century that shows this area bald as an egg.

Looking around, it was hard to believe what I was seeing. A dense green forest covers the entire crater. The rate at which the forest has overtaken bare rock is astonishing.

I walked around the rim of the cone to the high point of the island — a flat and rather unremarkable spot containing a picnic area and public toilets, as banal as a suburban kiddie playground. I could hardly imagine what it must have been like for the Māori living on the mainland nearby to have witnessed the sea erupt in steam, liquid fire shooting upwards in a column, turning the sky red, and a newborn mountain rising from the depths, right on this spot.

From the cone I took the long road home along a black track made of pulverized volcanic rock. It led to the lighthouse and beach at Mackenzie Point, and then back round to the ferry dock. Along the shore I noticed one other strange feature of the island: mangrove trees on the shoreline growing right out of the lava. This one has puzzled the scientists who study the island because mangroves typically grow in the muck of swampy wetlands. Here, they spring up directly from volcanic rubble. That was not thought to be possible for mangroves, at least until now.

All along the trail, I passed little wooden boxes with wire mesh sides; these are traps for possums and other invasive species that have made their way onto the island. They eat the eggs of native birds, so there's a concerted effort to cull the pests, and to keep them off the island. Visitors to the island are required to thoroughly check their knapsacks before they get on board the island ferry. The ferry attendant told us that in one case, they had caught a snake trying to smuggle aboard in someone's bag!

Even human pests have been removed from the island. As I neared the dock, I passed a stretch of shoreline with perhaps a dozen old cottages — the final remnant of a vacation community on Rangitoto in the early 1900s. All in all, there were 200 or so of these "baches," built over 100 years ago in ramshackle manner by the owners. Most of these have been dismantled, with just a few preserved, along with a small museum for the sake of history. These days, no one lives fulltime on the island — except the remaining pests, and the birds that helped create the forest. Including the tuneful tūi.

Rangitoto was my first taste of New Zealand outside of a city. So much of this country remains rugged and wild; yet all of it has been affected by humans. The unleashing of pets and pests upon this land — a land with no preexisting mammals — has created an imbalance that modern New Zealanders are belatedly striving hard to address. Most alarmingly, the numbers of kiwi, the national bird, are being reduced by 2% a year in unmanaged areas. So it's heartening to see the work being done in places like Rangitoto to repair the damage, and to find New Zealanders zealously embracing a new role on this island as protectors of life and observers of the amazing processes of Nature, as she unfolds her green hand upon this gray island.

Chapter 3

Russell: The Charming "Hellhole of the Pacific"

When the ships were in port and their crews loose on shore-leave, grogshops and brothels did a roaring trade. Life on the waterfront was rough, rowdy and sometimes violent, earning Kororāreka [Russell] the nickname *"hellhole of the Pacific"*.
— *Official website for the town of Russell*

Teresa chose the town of Russell as our first destination after Auckland. On the map, it is halfway up the Northland Peninsula — the northernmost, and hence warmest and most tropical, part of New Zealand — about a four-hour trip from the big city. Teresa described it to me as a quaint, historic port town. Little did I realize what a sordid reputation, and stunning history, this tiny cove community of 1000 souls has had.

The drive up State Highway 1 was a breeze, the road alternately passing though rolling green pastures and wild, forested hills. We dipped in towards the coast and strolled along white sand beaches by a turquoise sea. Indeed, New Zealand seemed like paradise (see page C1).

We arrived in Russell after dark, and so did not get a look at the town until our first morning. We had heard kiwi birds screeching to each other in the night. Stepping out onto the deck of our Air B&B, we could see below us sailboats moored in the little beach-fringed harbor, and beyond that, green islands in the blue bay. The whole area is as lush as a jungle. Birdsong filled the trees. Rains came and went, leaving rainbows hovering over the harbor.

The waterfront at Russell

The area is called the Bay of Islands, and it is probably among the first places the Māori saw, arriving in their sea canoes from Polynesia around a thousand years ago, according to archeological evidence. But the area was permanently settled only from the fifteenth century onwards. In 1769, the first European, Captain James Cook, arrived in his exploratory ship, the *Endeavour*. The captain spent ten days mapping the bay's 144 separate islands. That number has been officially reduced to 85, as the definition of "island" has become more strict: bare rocks poking above the waves no longer count; a proper island must have permanent vegetation (see page C2).

Captain Cook found dozens of Māori communities thriving all across the bay; he estimated 10,000 people in all. Cook easily traded with them for fresh food and supplies, and returned here on two subsequent journeys. He also spread the word about the bounty of the bay, and by the early 1800s, whaling ships were arriving to restock. Russell — then known by its Māori name, Kororāreka, which has the charming meaning, "Sweet Penguin," became the center of trade. Before long, it became the first permanent European settlement in all of New Zealand. A few enterprising Europeans (as well as some escaped convicts from Australia) decided to set up shop, catering to the whalers' other tastes — those "grogshops and brothels" the town website refers to.

Walking along the strand, it was hard for us to fathom that this charming little cove with its lush gardens and quaint homes had such an unsavory past. We stopped for our first meal at the Duke of Marlborough Hotel, right on the water's edge. In the lobby hangs a portrait of the original owner, Johnny Johnston, an Irish ex-convict who served his time in Australia then came to Kororāreka in 1826, where he opened the first grogshop in town — rum (grog) being most whalers' demon of choice. In a precocious bit of celebrity marketing, Johnny named his grogshop after the actual Duke of Marlborough, who was at the time the richest man in the world. The name has stuck through the centuries, even as the original pub was destroyed and later rebuilt as a hotel. It has belonged to nine different owners over the past 200 years. The walls reek of history, including Johnny's original liquor license, framed and proudly displayed.

Johnny Johnston's portrait, Duke of Marlborough Hotel

What I found most strange while visiting the museum and the various historical sites around Russell was that, according to artists' depictions, this lush cove was not at all green during the whaling years. The Māori cut down all the trees for masts and spars to sell to Europeans. I tried to imagine the land stripped bare, and added to that the vomit and excrement and trash that 500 drunken whalers must have produced every day during their shore leave — not to mention the brawls, violence, and ruined lives. Indeed, Sweet Penguin must have been an awful place. I later read that one of the several reasons the Māori wanted to sign a treaty with Britain was so there would be some legal authority to control the unruly Europeans, for there was no law to govern them in New Zealand. Kororāreka, "Hellhole of the Pacific," served as Exhibit A for the problem.

1840s artist's depiction of deforested Russell

Lush Russell today, from the same viewpoint

Much to the dismay of the local Māori chiefs who signed the Treaty of Waitangi in 1840, the following year the governor decided to move the capital from near Kororāreka to an area of land the government had purchased 150 miles south (to be named Auckland). Not only did all the officials relocate with the change, but the whalers moved their trade to the new port as well. The Kororāreka Māori chiefs were flabbergasted. Trade with the whalers had made them rich. Suddenly, all that wealth was taken away. It felt like a betrayal. Kororāreka became the site of much unrest as treaty promises were broken. By 1845, open hostilities had started in Kororāreka, resulting in the killing of some 20 British soldiers, the evacuation of the town, and subsequent bombardment of the Māori by a British warship.

This was the beginning of the New Zealand War between many Māori tribes and the *Pākehā* (European settler) government, a devastating conflict for the Māori that lasted for 28 years, until 1872. The entire economy of the Northland has never fully recovered. Auckland today has nearly 1.5 million people. Quiet little Russell is smaller than it was when Johnny opened his grogshop in 1826. But my oh my, little Sweet Penguin sure is lush and beautiful these days.

Chapter 4

Rainbow Falls, Kerikeri

Rainbow Falls — how could we resist visiting a park with such an evocative name?

The falls are in the little port town of Kerikeri on the Bay of Islands, about an hour's drive up the coast from our Air B&B in Russell. Weirdly enough, our map-app showed the falls were actually *inside* the town. We drove down a manicured suburban street, pulled into a parking lot with a park sign on it, and two minutes later found ourselves face to face with these crashing great falls. And whenever the sun shines on the spray, *voilà*, rainbows.

Actually, our first few weeks in New Zealand we discovered rainbows everywhere. This is because the country was having an unprecedentedly rainy year (resulting in horrific floods that had made world news the previous summer — doubtless influenced by climate change). Rainbows may seem like a nice side-effect, but rainbows, as I'm sure my astute readers well know, are an illusion. Rainbows are simply sunlight reflecting off water droplets. That's why a rainbow can never be reached, because it is an illusion that exists only in the observer's mind at a particular place and time.

At the base of Rainbow Falls we found a conservation area of endangered native kauri trees. A fungus known as the kauri-dieback is spreading through New Zealand, and so to enter the park we first had to scrub and wash our boots in little disinfectant baths at the entrance. Of course, the real reason this native evergreen is endangered is that it was too useful. The kauri has a tall straight trunk, which makes it ideal for boat-making, house-building, and carving; for over 100 years, kauri trees were felled wherever they stood. Today, kauri trees cover only 4% of their original habitat (see page C3).

Tim at Rainbow Falls. Is it raining?

The riverwalk below the falls eventually opens out into a grassy park, which is the site of the oldest permanent Christian mission in New Zealand. The mission house still stands. Built in 1822, it is the oldest wooden building in New Zealand. Right next door is the mission storehouse and trading center, built in

1830, which makes it the oldest *stone* building in the country. Both were constructed by the British Church Missionary Society to spearhead the conversion and "civilization" of the Māori people. Today, the Stone Store houses a museum on the second floor. In just a few spare rooms, the exhibit lays out the challenging, at times horrifying, tale of these first missionaries and their role in shaping the fate of New Zealand.

The Stone Store, the oldest stone building in New Zealand

These first evangelists were invited to the Bay of Islands by a powerful Māori chieftain who sold them land to set up their operations in Kerikeri for the price of 48 felling axes. Chief Hongi Hika was a soft-spoken man, known for his polite manners, and this helped him win the trust of Thomas Kendall, the head of the Christian mission. The two men became friends, each intrigued by the other's culture. Hongi Hika was an early adapter of European technology. He adopted new farming methods and grew new crops — particularly potatoes, which is what whaling ships most wanted to trade for when they reached the islands. Hongi Hika even encouraged Kendall to teach literacy and religion to his people, though the chief himself never converted to Christianity. Kendall warmed to the task. He set up the first school for Māori children. He learned the native language, *te reo Māori*, and was the first to transliterate it into the Roman alphabet. He went on to publish the first books in te reo Māori.

Kendall and Hongi Hika traveled together to Sydney in 1814. While there, the chief studied not just agriculture, but also military strategy. He returned home with muskets and ammunition. It turned out Hongi Hika was also an early adapter of European methods of warfare, for he had grasped all too well that British "civilization" was not really about religion: it was about exerting power through violence. Te Māori (the name the Māori people give themselves) were a warrior culture, but their battles were close fought, hand to hand, with whalebone choppers and wooden spears for thrusting. This actually kept bloodshed to a minimum, and gave tribes a good reason to try diplomacy first when settling disputes. Muskets changed everything. Armed with muskets, Hongi Hika's tribe easily defeated their enemies with minimal losses to their own forces. As his territory grew, he hungered for more. The missionaries were appalled when war parties would return home to Kerikeri with prisoners of war, and then *cannibalized* them.

Because the missionaries had no land to cultivate, they had no option but to trade with Hongi Hika's tribe for food. When the chief suddenly decided to trade only for muskets, the Christians were faced with a devil's bargain. They needed food to live and do the Lord's work. But the price they paid was aiding and abetting war. Kendall himself defended Hongi Hika, arguing the mission was in no position to dictate terms of trade to their Māori protectors.

In 1820, Kendell again accompanied Hongi Hika abroad, this time to London, where the chief's facial tattoos made him the talk of the town. He met King George, gained many influential friends, and collected many valuable gifts — which on the chief's return via Sydney he promptly traded for 300 muskets plus ammunition. Hongi Hika landed in New Zealand ready for conquest. He took the land of other tribes and made slaves of the defeated. The slaves were forced to farm their former land in order to produce cash crops, which Hongi Hika then sold to Europeans to buy more muskets. Soon he had over 1000 guns and a huge army. Other tribes began to arm themselves in defense. Learning from Hongi Hika's example, they also attacked *their* enemies before they got guns, too. This unprecedented tribal violence cascaded throughout all of New Zealand.

This bloody period of Māori history is called "The Musket Wars." It lasted for 22 years, from 1818 to 1840. Eventually, every tribe managed to procure muskets and learned how to build fortified defenses against musket attacks. The initial advantage of the new weapon was neutralized, and the tribes, exhausted from killing one another, eventually stopped fighting. Out of a total population of about 100,000, it's estimated at least 20,000 Māori died in the Musket Wars. Most of them would have been young men, the warriors. Whole tribes were displaced, local industries ruined. The fabric of Māori society was shredded.

Hongi Hika was shot in the chest during a battle in 1827; he died of his infected wounds 14 months later. According to one account, the chief warned his people on his deathbed that, if "red coat" British soldiers should ever land in New Zealand, "when you see them make war against them." His words proved prophetic. The next generation saw widespread warfare between the weakened and disparate tribes and British soldiers, and much death. In the end, it meant defeat for Te Māori.

One has to wonder: what would have happened if, instead of attacking other tribes and creating civil war, Hongi Hika had united his people and used his military prowess against the British? New Zealand would be a different place today.

Chapter 5

A Fierce Māori Welcome in Waitangi

The Māori warrior ran towards me from the entrance of his ceremonial meeting place. He approached with his spear held high over his shoulder, eyes bulging menacingly. He yelled, but I knew not to flinch, and definitely not to turn my back on him. I was in his territory, and there was a right way to do this and a wrong way, so I had been instructed. He stopped a few feet away from me and glared. He twirled his spear like a kung-fu master. He was tall, much taller than the others, young and lithe.

"Ou!" he grunted at me loudly. "Ou! Ou!"

Not taking his eyes from me, he bent down. From beneath his robe, he pulled out a leafy twig and set it on the ground.

My response to his offering would determine whether we would be treated as friends who come in peace, or as enemies who must be fought. Māori warrior culture developed around the need to protect their territory from aggressive neighbors. And so, this test of visitors coming into their space has been formalized into a ritual welcome ceremony designed to reveal the intentions of a visitor. Fortunately, I had been told exactly what to do. I stepped forward, knelt and picked up the offered leaves, then backed up, slowly, in the direction of my own tribe.

My "tribe" had chosen me not two minutes earlier to be their chief. When I say "chosen," I mean the Māori woman who was initiating the group of us tourists into the welcome ceremony had asked for a volunteer to represent us as a tribe. We 30-odd visitors to Waitangi shuffled our feet and looked about, seeing if anyone had the nerve to raise a hand. Teresa, standing next to me, pointed her elbow at me and tilted her head sideways in my direction. Our Māori hostess caught the gesture. Her eyes lit up, and she beckoned me forward. I looked at Teresa. My beloved smiled at me. I could read all too well the words behind the glint in her eyes: *Oh you are going to love this! Don't pretend you're not...*

And so, twig in hand, I rejoined my tribe while the Māori warrior sprinted back and rejoined the other members of his tribe, who were waiting by the entrance of the hall. Then they sang and danced a ritual invitation to enter their sacred, communal space.

As we walked towards the entrance, our Māori hostess told me: "After our chief gives a speech to welcome your tribe, *you* must give a speech in response, on behalf of your tribe. It should be no longer than our chief's speech, but no shorter either. Five minutes max would be good."

There was an audible gasp from the members of my new tribe as they heard this. They threw me shocked and pained expressions of pity and compassion. I knew they were thinking, "Oh, thank *God* I didn't volunteer!"

Now, there are some things I am afraid of: a tall man rushing at me with a spear; sharks (at least when I'm swimming in deep water); hornets; playing a musical instrument on a stage. But one thing I am most emphatically not afraid of is giving an impromptu speech to a room full of strangers. Heck, for a living I *teach* environmentalists and economists and government leaders how to give good speeches. So, walking to the front of the stage, I was already mapping out the structure of my talk and deciding on my main message.

Teresa, as the chief's wife, was invited to sit front and center. She whispered to me as I walked by her towards the stage: "See. I *knew* you were going to love this."

The Māori chief began his speech, almost bellowing at us in te reo Māori. He was a large man, in that Polynesian way that appears massive without looking out of shape. He gestured aggressively, shaking his spear at us. Although this was a cultural performance, it seemed very intense, very genuine, whatever he was saying. Suddenly he switched to English. "We hope you all enjoy the show!" he told us with a broad smile.

Then he motioned to me to take center stage and speak.

Friends of mine who hear this tale might be amazed that indeed I kept my speech to under five minutes. But I kept our training principles in mind (*Rule number one: never go over your alloted time*). After all, we were here to watch the performance, not listen to a TED Talk (*Rule number two: the speaker is in service to the audience*). But I was also struck by how wholeheartedly our Māori hosts were playing their roles, not simply going through the motions, but making it real. So I was determined to play my assigned part as well as I could (*Rule number three: deliver the goods*). This is the gist of what I said:

"Thank you for welcoming us into this sacred space... We are a new tribe, and have come together from many faraway nations. What unites us as a tribe is our curiosity. We are here to learn about your people. We do not want to learn only from books, or the Internet. We want to learn directly from you, our gracious hosts. We know you are here to share your culture with us, your traditions, and your history. We know that you are opening your hearts to us. And I tell you, *my* tribe is here with open hearts to receive the gifts that you share with us today. Thank you."

Everyone seemed well pleased with that, and I took my seat next to Teresa as the show began (see page C4).

The performance included traditional songs (with explanations in English) of how the Māori ancestors came here by sea canoe from Polynesia, ritual dances, hand-to-hand combat demonstrations with spears and choppers, as well as explanations of the meaning of various carvings and adornments on the weapons. Those colorful feathers bunched behind the spear tip? They are both decorative and practical. If the blow lands, they soak up the blood and prevent the spear handle from getting slippery during battle. The troupe showed us the whimsical side of Māori life as well. They played traditional games, with swinging balls and passing sticks, tossing them back and forth with mesmerizing precision. It was for us a beautiful introduction to Māori culture and history at Waitangi.

When it was over and our raucous applause died down, Teresa and I were invited on stage first to get our pictures taken with the performers, who displayed a good sense of fun trying to teach us how to make the Māori warrior expression of fierce defiance: tongue out, eyes bulging wide. Unfortunately, as the photo below makes all too clear, Teresa resembles a defiant toddler, and I look as if I have just sat on a spear point, right up to the feathers!

Oh dear, the travelers' tribal chief and Mrs. chief look ridiculous.

We left the meeting hall and headed to an old bungalow further down the path. This house is the reason Waitangi is famous in New Zealand, and it's why we came here to this green hill, about a three-hour drive north from Auckland. This is the place where, in 1840, the Treaty of Waitangi was signed between some 50 Māori chiefs and the representative of the King of England, confirming New Zealand would become a new British colony. The treaty was then sent all around the islands to each tribe, and was eventually signed by over 500 chiefs. It became the founding document of the nation — but also the source of much misunderstanding, strife, and bloodshed.

The Treaty of Waitangi was drafted in two languages, English and te reo Māori, but very few of those who signed could read both languages. This was a problem, because there were fundamental differences between the two versions. The English treaty stated the Māori were ceding *sovereignty* over the land to the British, who in return were granting the native people the rights to their traditional lands and to self-government. The te reo Māori version said the British Crown would make laws to govern and control the British settlers who were becoming unruly on the islands, and would protect the rights of Te Māori. The treaty did not even use the well-known Māori word for sovereignty, *rangatiratanga*.

Left: Hone Heke, the first chief to sign the Treaty of Waitangi, and one who cut down the British flagpole at Russell in response to treaty violations. Right: Canoes gathering at Waitangi. (My photos from the Russell Museum)

And so, in the years following the signing, as the British acted more and more as if they were in charge, many Māori began to object. In defiance, Hone Heke, the Māori chief who first signed the treaty, cut down the flagpole in nearby Kororāreka (Russell) which flew the British flag. The British put a new pole up again. But three times more, the Māori cut it down. The last felling of the flag set off a battle in which many soldiers were killed, the town was evacuated, and a British ship in the harbor then bombarded and destroyed the place!

In the years that followed, the British violated the treaty again and again, particularly with the illegal appropriation of Māori land. Wars broke out between Pākehā communities and Māori. The British, of course, had the empire on their side. From time to time British warships and troops were called in, leaving the Māori outnumbered and outgunned in their homeland. In short, they lost. More European settlers moved in, and over the next century the Māori became a minority — dispossessed, disempowered, and disillusioned.

What is most amazing, though, is that 50 years ago, in the 1970s, when a new generation of Māori leaders began protesting for justice, they had the Treaty of Waitangi they could turn to, to demand their legal rights. Pākehā New Zealanders, after years of ignoring the treaty, began to listen, and began to feel a sense of accountability for past wrongs their ancestors had committed.

And so, in 1975, the Government of New Zealand passed the Treaty of Waitangi Act, "to provide for the observance, and confirmation, of the principles of the Treaty of Waitangi by establishing a Tribunal to make recommendations on claims relating to the practical application of the Treaty and to determine whether certain matters are inconsistent with the principles of the Treaty."

The tribunal not only investigated and ruled on treaty violations, but also awarded compensation and damages, and

31

has done so dozens of times. For example, in 1995 the tribunal ruled that the state had to pay compensation of $170 million to the Tainui tribe for violating their treaty rights. This was accompanied by an unprecedented royal apology from Queen Elizabeth, who delivered it in person in New Zealand. Many other Māori tribes, however, remain unhappy with their compensation, and not all treaty violations have been resolved.

In 2014, the tribunal actually ruled that the *Māori never conceded their sovereignty in the 1840 treaty*. The ramifications of this are still being worked out, and the history of New Zealand, as a land of two peoples, one nation, is far from finished.

Chapter 6

Rotorua: From Hell's Gate to Craters of the Moon

Many lakes in the center of New Zealand's North Island are circular in shape for a very simple reason: they are calderas of volcanic eruptions from ages past. A caldera is the inside of a crater, and so to stroll along the shores of these lakes is to walk the rim of a volcano.

Teresa and I spent three days by each of the two largest of these lakes, Rotorua and Taupō. Taupō is the largest lake in New Zealand. Its volcano erupted massively in about AD 260, blowing 19 cubic kilometers (4.5 cubic miles) of matter into the sky. That would be the equivalent of 7600 Great Pyramids of Giza shot into the atmosphere. It was the greatest eruption Earth had experienced in over 5000 years. People as far away as Japan would have noticed their sunsets and sunrises were particularly vivid that year, as dust from the eruption swirled far across the Pacific.

These lakes were too big for me to really "get" their volcanic nature. Stocked with trout, and featuring boat cruises and kayak tours, with black swans and ducks paddling about, I couldn't wrap my head around the fact they are actually the mouths of violent eruptions. It was easier for me to feel the closeness of the molten magma beneath our feet in the region's thermal parks. These feature bubbling hot springs, fumaroles venting steam, and hot mud pits. They are all on Māori land, and each has its own unique geology, tribal lore, and marketing approach. We visited three of these very different parks while by the lakes.

Hell's Gate

Located on the far side of Lake Rotorua, away from most of the town's tourist attractions, there's no doubt the provocative name draws people to this steamy hellscape. Teresa and I smelled the sulfur from the parking lot. The local Māori *iwi* (tribe), Ngāti Rangiteaorere, who own and operate the park, have constructed a walkway through this portion of their territory filled with bubbling mud pits.

When underground rivers flow into thermal areas, the water turns to steam. If steam rises up through water, you get hot springs. If steam rises up through fissures in the rock, you get fumaroles. And if steam rises up through clay and volcanic ash deposits, it liquifies into mud, and looks like pools of bubbling chocolate pudding, but gray.

"Bubbling Mud Pits" might not have drawn the crowds, so I wondered: who was the PR genius who came up with "Hell's Gate"? It was none other than George Bernard Shaw, who visited the site while touring New Zealand in 1934. There's a large plaque in his honor in the park, and some of the other steaming mud pits bear the names Shaw gave to them, such as "Sodom and Gomorrah." How wise of the tribe not to choose that one as the park's name.

Hell's Gate: mud pits and Shavian wit everywhere

As well as the walk through hell, the park features a spa where you can soak in the hot mud. Yum! According to the Hell's Gate website:

As you walk through native bush and clouds of geothermic steam, you'll discover why this land has inspired myths and legends. Once used by Māori warriors to heal their battle-scarred bodies, visitors now use the nutrient-rich waters and mud to ease inflammation and arthritis, as well as rejuvenate the skin. This unique blend of awe-inspiring power and natural healing properties is a thing of cultural legend — having been used for over 800 years.

The website features photos of a loving, mud-smeared couple embracing in a muddy pool. Such fun they are having! Teresa was… not convinced.

"I could not imagine anything worse than getting hot mud into all kinds of crevices," she opined, delicately.

Now, according to my intensive Internet research on the subject, the minerals and volcanic residue in the mud are antibacterial. However, while mud baths do no harm, there's not much scientific evidence to back up the claimed health benefits. Except for stress relief, which is indeed significant as the muscles of the body relax into the soothing, hot mud. That relaxation was clearly *not* going to occur if I had to wrestle Teresa into the sulfuric soup and struggle to hold her down while she wriggled about. So we gave it a miss.

Whakarewarewa Living Māori Village and Thermal Park

Just on the outskirts of the town of Rotorua is Whakarewarewa, home of the Tūhourangi Ngāti Wāhiao iwi, who built their homes in the midst of these thermal hot springs several hundred years ago. For the past 200 years, they have opened their village to visiting Europeans who come to have a look, curious about the bubbling pools and the people who make their homes in their midst.

The self-guided walk through the park takes one through parts of the quiet little village. Signs posted here and there request visitors not to intrude on the privacy of residents. Markers along the way explain the various uses of the bubbling pools: some are for bathing, while the hottest ones are for cooking. Given Rotorua's cool winter temperatures, I realized what an amazing discovery these hot pools must have been to the first tribes to arrive in the area. Hot water ready at your doorstep, every day of the year (see page C6)!

Hot springs at Whakarewarewa Village

Early on, the village realized they had something special for visitors. In the 1800s a tradition developed for tribal women to guide foreigners through the thermal wonders of the wider area.

The museum next to the village does not explain why it was the women who were the guides. Perhaps the men were busy with farming and other, more steady work; perhaps guiding tourists was beneath the status of men; or perhaps women learned English more readily? Whatever the reason, women guides became well reputed in the area, increasing the iwi's income and ultimately the status of the women, who became quite revered, even famous.

Although the tourist trade allowed the tribe to prosper, contact with outsiders brought in diseases. Influenza, measles, and other epidemics wiped out a quarter of the tribe by 1900. Meanwhile, court rulings stripped 83% of the Tūhourangi Ngāti Wāhiao iwi's traditional land away from them. The New Zealand government even sought to regulate guiding in those years. During this contentious period, the state wanted to ban women from guiding altogether, but they persevered and the tradition of women guides continued well into the twentieth century.

Today, as well as guided tours, the iwi offers cultural experiences, a small museum, and a gift shop. But one would hardly describe this little village as prosperous, compared to the shiny downtown streets of Rotorua right next door, with its chic restaurant district and well-manicured parks. As we have heard, again and again since arriving in New Zealand, "poverty remains a persistent problem among the Māori..."

Craters of the Moon

Just north of Lake Taupō, Craters of the Moon takes visitors on a walk through a very different landscape. No bubbling pools, just steaming ground on a wide-open landscape. The heat destabilizes the surface, so that over time, here and there it has collapsed into craters, large and small. A wooden walkway runs through the park. Signs along the route warn visitors not to step off the path, because the ground might disintegrate right beneath your feet.

One of many "Craters of the Moon" near Taupō

It's an eerie feeling to put your hand on the ground and feel the heat rise up. Other signs informed us that just 10–30 centimeters (4–12 inches) below the surface, the temperature is more than 98 degrees Celsius (208 °F) in places — just shy of boiling. That means the plants that grow here are well-adapted to a hot climate, with tough, heat-resistant leaves and roots. Some mosses that thrive inside the craters are usually found in hot, tropical climates.

Right next to the park is a geothermal power plant which pumps surface water underground, generating steam and turning turbines for the town of Taupō. From the thermal park we could see the gleaming metal pipes in the distance. Geothermal power provides about 20% of New Zealand's power these days, with the potential for much more. Especially in an era of climate change, there's a great opportunity for the country to transform into a net-zero nation through the natural power of the Earth.

***

Walking through these three geothermal parks filled me with a kind of reverence for the Earth. To feel the hot magma beneath our planet's skin made it seem alive in a way that was both frightening and exhilarating. The Māori have their own story about this tremendous force, as told on the Hell's Gate website:

> Rūaumoko is the God of earthquakes, volcanoes and seasons. As the son of the sky father, Ranginui, and the earth mother, Papatūānuku, his legend begins with their separation. Rūaumoko was taken by his mother to keep her company in a world below our own. The gift bestowed on him was fire, to keep them both warm. It is said that with every movement he makes, Rūaumoko's heat boils the earth above.

I felt Rūaumoko in the heat beneath my feet. There have been 17 episodes of volcanic unrest in New Zealand since 1872. Most recently, in December 2019, 22 people lost their lives and 25 others were seriously injured as a result of the eruption of the nearby Whakaari volcano (White Island, just off the coast), while it was being visited by tour groups.

What about Taupō itself? What would happen if it were to erupt? As the website www.groundreport.in explains:

> Most of the North Island of New Zealand would be covered in sulphurous ash that would kill everything. There would have been a few days' warning, but not enough capacity to get everyone off the island in that time. The North Island of New Zealand would be suffocated under a thick blanket of smoke and lava. Chunks of rock and ash would rain down from the sky, likely causing more tragedies.

So... not good. But the same website optimistically adds:

> A 2020 paper published in *Earth and Planetary Science Letters* put the annual odds of such an eruption occurring

over the next 500 years between 0.5 and 1.3 per cent. The magma needs more time to build up before there is likely to be superimposition.

They conclude, however, that a lot more work needs to go into the science of monitoring Taupō.

Just to unravel the math: a 1% *annual chance* of an eruption in the next 500 years means *every year there is a one-in-a-hundred chance*. Which is a little less comforting. Rūaumoko remains unpredictable.

Chapter 7

Tongariro Alpine Pass: The Trail to Mount Doom

From the bay window of our rental condo on the shores of Lake Taupō, we could see a range of volcanoes rising up from the far side of the lake's great caldera, some 100 kilometers (60 miles) away, their cones covered in snow in the southern winter months. Cold and impressive, these giants are far from extinct. A painting in the Taupō museum shows one of them, Ngauruhoe, still smoking in 1870. There's also a museum photo of Ngauruhoe erupting in 1926. In fact, Ngauruhoe is the most active volcano in all of New Zealand, with 45 eruption events recorded in the twentieth century.

Left: Ngauruhoe and his "brothers" as seen from the town of Taupō. Right: A 1926 photo of Ngauruhoe erupting, from the Taupō library (Neville Hoy collection)

The mountain's name means "Throwing Hot Stones." Ngauruhoe plays a central role in the defining Māori myth of the area. The ancestor-chief who first reached the shores of Lake Taupō found the place deadly cold. So he summoned volcanic fire from Hawaiki, the mythic homeland, which emerged at Ngauruhoe.

Surprisingly, Ngauruhoe also played a role in an important Western cultural myth: it was the stand-in for scenes of Mount Doom in the *Lord of the Rings* trilogy, which was filmed in New Zealand. While the Hobbits were able to climb Mount Doom and destroy the accursed ring in its molten crater, alas, in real life, one is not allowed to do so. Due to the mountain's sacred nature for Te Māori, walking on Ngauruhoe is forbidden (sorry, Frodo!). Instead, there is a hike that threads a path up a valley next to Ngauruhoe, across the saddle to nearby Mount Tongariro, and then descends on the other side. The hike is 19 kilometers (12 miles) long, takes about eight hours, and is reputed to be the best one-day hike in New Zealand.

In wintertime the local tourist bureau actively discourages people from doing the Tongariro Crossing without special training, full mountaineering gear, and a guide. At age 64, I was a bit too old for all that. But, as this was the only time I was ever going to be in New Zealand, I thought I might as well walk the first part of the trail, up the valley to the flank of Mount Ngauruhoe.

I dressed warmly, took all my rain gear, and headed out for the day. Ninety minutes later, I arrived at the trailhead at the end of a gravel road. The large parking lot was totally empty except for one other car. There were several empty bus bays, and I could tell that during the summer months this route must be packed with hikers. But not today. A big sign warned — and I paraphrase it here:

Do not do this hike in winter! Unless:

- You are trained and experienced in winter mountain climbing
- You are trained in avalanche awareness

- You have an emergency geolocator beacon in case you get buried by an avalanche
- You have a death wish

Okay, I made up the last bullet, but that was the general tone of the sign. I checked zero of these boxes, but I wasn't too worried because I only intended to walk part of the way, and if the trail was clear of snow, maybe climb to the saddle before heading back down. I had even packed my new hiking poles, just to be on the safe side. The weather was overcast when I started, but not raining. I put on my rain pants and jacket and headed up the valley.

This moment is always the sweetest: starting along an unknown path on an empty trail into the wilderness. The vegetation was scrubby and tough, much of it russet-red in the dead of winter (see page C7). There was a wind at my back, which made walking all the easier. No more than a few hundred meters along the trail, I passed two guys walking the other way (they were too tall to be Hobbits). That was obviously their car in the parking lot. It was 1 p.m. and they were finishing their hike while I was just starting out. The sun would set at five. With a bit of a qualm, I realized I would be truly alone on the mountain for the rest of the afternoon. Then it began to rain.

As the trail rose, white daubs of snow appeared on the sides of the valley. Then streaks and patches. After about an hour, the landscape looked like a calico cat, with mottled patches of red, white, and black. Fortunately, the track here was on a raised wooden walkway, covered with a steel grid, easy to grip with my boots. But the weather was getting worse. The rain picked up, and visibility deteriorated. I could still see enough of the walls of the valley to be confident there was no accumulation of snow, so no chance of an avalanche. Then I hit this signpost:

43

Mount Doom looking pretty doom-ish

Notice that this instruction is for summer weather, and it advises "TURN BACK!" if the weather is cloudy — let alone rainy, windy, and foggy. But again, I was not going to the top, just out for an afternoon stroll. So, onward.

The trail kept rising, the valley narrowing. Wooden steps climbed to a higher valley that was icy cold, and purely breathtaking. Big black lumps of misshapen rock cluttered the land. A sign next to the trail explained that during the more recent eruptions of Mount Ngauruhoe, lava flowed down this valley floor. I imagined what this day might have looked like back then: fire and ice, with steam rising hot as the cold rain fell on the flowing magma. Looking up, across the valley floor to where fresh snow covered the rising slope, I knew I had reached the base of Mount Doom. I was at the foot of Ngauruhoe, but I could not see it.

The rain was really coming on strong by this time, and the wind at my back was howling. The walls of the valley form a wind funnel here, so I had read, that gathers force and velocity to well over 60 miles per hour (95 km/h). Fortunately, I had brought my new, most-favored hiking companion: a sturdy folding umbrella. I deployed it now to keep my head and torso relatively dry; holding it open at my back, I could feel the wind push me forward up the trail.

I thought, why not make it to the end of the valley, where the trail climbs the slope towards the saddle? It was a bit slippy-slidey on the icy part of the walkway. Not a big deal, so long as I didn't fall off and twist an ankle. All alone, well out of cell service, there would be no one coming to my rescue today. I corrected that thought: rather than picturing myself twisting an ankle, better to visualize placing each step firmly and surely, staying aware and taking my time with each step.

I followed the walkway to where it ended in a marshy bowl. A mucky trail followed the stream for a while, gradually deteriorating into a wandering line of deep, snow-covered bootprints through the snowfield. They led to where the climb up the saddle began. Oh, I sorely wanted to go there. But the snow ahead was knee deep, and soon I would be post-holing through it, possibly breaking through into marshy water. Ahead, the steep sides of the narrowed valley were accumulating snow, enough that an avalanche might be possible. It was time to call it quits.

I thought of Sam. I thought of Frodo. They did not turn back. They pushed on! But they had a mission. They had a world to save. I was just a flâneur out for a ramble alone where perhaps he should not be. Plus, it was not *raining* when the Hobbits climbed Mount Doom.

Umbrella towards the wind, the walk back to the parking lot was like tacking a sailboat into a gale. I had to lean into it. I couldn't hold the umbrella into the wind for long, as it put a lot of strain on the outstretched arm. So I propped the handle against my chest like a mast and pointed the umbrella horizontally into oncoming rain. Whenever the angle slipped just a little bit, the whole thing would whirl around and plop inside out, jerking me around with it.

The tops of my boots were wet now from rain running down my legs. My feet were soaked. My rain pants were no longer waterproof. They were drenched and starting to sag with the extra weight. Every hundred steps or so, I would have to hitch them up so they wouldn't slip down to my knees, like some old man who had forgotten his belt. I was pretty sure I looked ridiculous on this long, slow, soggy retreat from the volcano. Mr. Mature Flâneur, mythic action-adventure figure: not cautious enough to stay home; not foolish enough to climb into danger; but just barely wise enough to know when to turn around.

Chapter 8

Napier: Art Deco Capital of the World

Teresa and I wanted to visit the beachside town of Napier, on the east coast of New Zealand's North Island, for the strangest of reasons. A massive earthquake destroyed the town in 1931, killing 256 people. But from the rubble, the town rebuilt itself in the then-new architectural trend of Art Deco. We both love Art Deco, and we were most curious to see a whole town done up in this style.

According to the Napier city website, "Art Deco expressed all the vigor and optimism of the roaring twenties, and the idealism and escapism of the grim thirties." Napier threw itself into reconstruction with the goal of becoming the most modern town in the world. But it also wanted to rebuild earthquake safe: two-story buildings with reinforced concrete, which well suited the angular, streamlined look of Art Deco. The façades were decorated with Art Deco's signature geometric designs and intricate patterns — including some that mimicked Māori motifs. As a result, Napier today has the highest concentration of Art Deco buildings anywhere and claims to be the Art Deco Capital of the World.

Yeah... Nah (as New Zealanders are prone to saying — a way of sounding agreeable while disagreeing). Surely that can't be true? When Art Deco came of age it was all the rage in major cities across the US and Europe. What about New York? What about Miami? Paris? New Zealanders were, in my month-long experience, a rather self-effacing lot. They were modest. Heck, they said "sorry" almost more than Canadians. So was Napier's Art Deco *hutzpah* really warranted?

I did some research. *Architectural Digest* confirmed it. They started their list of "Top Ten Art Deco Cities" (August 2016) with Napier. The *Smithsonian Magazine* also verified the claim: "How an Earthquake Turned This New Zealand Town into the Art Deco Capital of the World" (February 2016).

The key word, of course, is *concentration*. Miami has six times more Art Deco buildings than Napier's 140, but Miami's are spread out through the city. Napier is a compact little town, especially the downtown business area where most of the Art Deco buildings can be seen within an hour's walk. So yes, Napier has the greatest *concentration* of Art Deco buildings in the world. It is actually the experience of walking down entire blocks of Art Deco buildings that makes Napier a unique place to visit, irresistible to a couple of global flâneurs like Teresa and me.

The drive to Napier took us through the mountains above Hawke's Bay on the eastern coast. As we descended the river valley we were appalled by the wreckage: houses torn from their foundations, cars bent and broken by the roadside, train tracks twisted like a rollercoaster, and everywhere mud and debris. With a shock, we realized these were the remains of Napier's most recent natural disaster.

In February 2023, Cyclone Gabrielle deluged New Zealand's northeast coast, causing mudslides and lethal flooding. It hit Napier hard, wiping out roads, bridges, power, and the sanitation system, leaving tens of thousands without basic services for weeks. Further down the highway, we saw entire vineyards and orchards still covered in mud and waste, the vines and trees broken and dead. It was heartbreaking.

Despite the destruction, the town center of Napier was high enough to have avoided the worst of the floods. A peculiar fact: the 1931 earthquake *elevated* the land by 3 full meters (10 feet). The uplift drained the lagoon and left former beachfront properties about 50 meters (160 feet) from the shore. The earthquake thus helped raise the town above the worst of Gabrielle's floodwaters when it hit in 2023.

Cyclone Gabrielle: after the mudslide

Our little B&B was one of those houses formerly by the shore. This building survived the 1931 earthquake because it was built of sturdy wooden beams and not brick like much of the town center. The old house has been lovingly brought back to life by the new owners, Tom and Esther Seymour. Teresa tells me she knew from the photos on the website that this place was special, which is why she booked us there.

Tom and Esther were special, too. We stay mostly at hotels and Air B&Bs as we travel. While we have polite conversations at check-in and check-out, we don't really get to know people. So small B&Bs are a nice chance for a more personal connection with our hosts. But we have rarely met a couple who made us feel so welcome in their home. From the moment we arrived, we felt like old friends who had come to visit. Esther and Tom served us afternoon tea, then we sat and chatted for an hour or so, honestly, as if we were catching up rather than meeting for the first time.

When we parted, they invited us for a five o'clock glass of wine before we headed off for dinner. It was not plonk, either! Hawke's Bay is one of the finest wine-growing regions in New Zealand, and I am convinced the locals keep the good stuff for themselves. The day we left they casually told us they were being interviewed by the local paper for having won the "Rising Star Award" from the National B&B Association of New Zealand. They sure deserve it (www.415marineparade.co.nz).

Our Napier hosts (and new friends) Esther and Tom

In all, we had only one sunny day in Napier. We were determined to *carpe* that *diem* and flâner along all the Art Deco streets in the town center. Armed with a map that numbered each building and provided some background, we began to zigzag through the downtown core. It was like going back in time... but tidier. Most of the old buildings have been restored and repainted in the past decade or so. They looked all shiny and new (see pages C8–C9).

We wandered around in a happy daze, for the buildings all seemed fresh, the colors bright, the lines clean and crisp, with flourishes of geometrical forms — chevrons and trapezoids, perfect curves and tight repeating patterns. Some Art Deco buildings were grand department stores a full block long. Others were banks, the museum, the art gallery, the former office of the *New Zealand Herald*. I found myself especially drawn to the small stores and cafés that not only preserved the old façades but also added Art Deco signage and refurbished interiors. We also discovered some quirky juxtapositions. For example, the grand-looking Australian Mutual Provident Society building with its fancy brass-handled double door, columns, and gold-leaf molding is currently home to the Blue Lagoon Tattoo Studio.

We found posters everywhere announcing the annual Napier Art Deco Festival was coming the third week of July, and we regretted that we were going to miss it. Tom and Esther told us people come from all over New Zealand, and even overseas, for the event. They dress up in the high style of the Roaring Twenties and attend fancy dances and period-themed dinners in costume. Some people arrive in vintage cars, and the town throws itself into a frenzy of nostalgia. If you are in New Zealand in July, I can only encourage you to make the effort to join in the fun.

But before you slip on your tux or flapper dress and pearls, I would also recommend taking a look at a thoughtful and eloquent PhD thesis by New Zealander Franky Strachan: *Veneers and Facades: A Re-evaluation of the Status and Meaning of Napier's Art Deco*. I found it while rummaging around the Internet. I contacted the author and she gave me permission to quote her work. The author "approaches Napier's Art Deco as ... an ongoing visual-cultural production" and asks "Who are we that *this* is Napier? Why does Napier look like this, *now*?" Her answer is not an easy one, so I will interpret (see my paraphrase below):

Art Deco culture does not represent racial, economic, gender, or body diversity because the imagery is drawn from an era of prejudiced class privilege [Art Deco's upper-class American and European roots]. Where the past is excessively simulated, visitors are less likely to be moved by the historical sensation. Yet when historical objects and sites are presented in their primary form their evocations tend to be more innately compelling.

In presenting heritage, we must therefore preserve the *metonym* (the temporal and contextual otherness of historic artifacts) while selling the *metaphor* (the mediated experience).

— Franky Strachan, *Veneers and Facades: A Re-evaluation of the Status and Meaning of Napier's Art Deco*, Academia. edu, 2019 (italics mine)

To paraphrase as simply as I can: It's easy to get swept up in Napier's Art Deco-ness. But that makes it too easy to sweep everything else about Napier's past under the carpet. While the glitzy version of the town's transformation into a city of the future (now frozen in the past) takes center stage, other narratives of the town's history have been pushed into the background.

As if in response to Franky's provocation, the nearby Hawke's Bay Tai Ahuriri Museum provides a different set of perspectives on the region's past. I spent a rainy afternoon there. The first floor contains an exhibit that tells "a history of people and places of Ngāti Kahungunu, telling stories of their time and the events that shaped Te Matau-a-Māui into the region of Hawke's Bay, events that also helped to shape Aotearoa into New Zealand."

The common theme of the exhibit was the Māori struggles with the government over land sales, mostly during the second half of the nineteenth century. More than a decade after the signing of the Treaty of Waitangi in 1840, the new government was pressuring them to sell tribal land so that more settlers could move in. Māori land was held, collectively, by each iwi. Though individual tribe members sometimes wanted to sell, the chiefs would often reject the offers outright for the good of the community.

Then in 1865, the government passed a new law decreeing land could not be owned by more than ten persons, effectively voiding the collective tribal ownership, making land sales easier, but breaking the terms of the treaty. The museum exhibit documents one case near Napier in which the government simply threw a Māori iwi off its territory in order to build a golf course. They were, however, "offered the opportunity to play golf on the course for free."

To put it very bluntly, the exhibit makes clear that for the Māori in Hawke's Bay, the 1931 earthquake was not the worst disaster. Their worst disaster was the recurring violation of treaty agreements with the Crown that resulted in the loss of their land and their way of life.

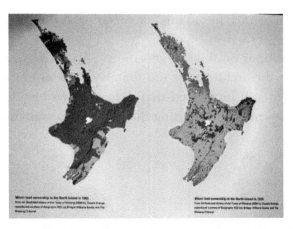

My photo from the Wellington Te Papa Museum showing the Māori loss of land in New Zealand's North Island between 1860 and 1939

The exhibit is solemn, the room dark. Large photos of the elders accompany the text that tells their stories, in English and te reo Māori. What amazes me is not that there are narratives of the British betraying and impoverishing the indigenous people of this land; that's the story of colonialization everywhere. But rather, how this story is being told in Napier and in other places I have visited in New Zealand: in the voices of the Māori, in museums that are clearly curated by Te Māori.

Teresa put it well. She said to me, "The difference between New Zealand and North America is that here there's a *conversation* going on."

I checked back with Franky, and she wrote to me:

While Maori cultural representation is present at the museum and other curated private spaces, it is not part of the daily "place ballet" of Napier. As you noted, Napier's Art Deco contrivance is an ongoing choice, and an ongoing cultural production. This underrepresentation is also true of other marginalised groups that belong to Napier, and if the museum exhibit is the best response the local council has to this conversation, it is not enough.

As an interloper on this conversation — a flâneur who listens as much to the architecture and the museums as to the spoken word — I'm still impressed that at least some people on both sides are listening, and finding the dialogue worthwhile.

Chapter 9

Te Mata Peak and the Story of Sheep

Climbing to Te Mata Peak felt glorious. The sky was clear. The sun was warm. The strong wind cooled the air just enough to keep me from sweating. It only took an hour to hike from the park trailhead to the summit. And what a staggering view! To the west, grassy green-and-beige hills undulate far into the distant horizon. To the east, the long spine of Te Mata stretches out towards Hawke's Bay on New Zealand's eastern coast and beyond to the South Pacific (see page C10).

The mountain itself is a long, limestone escarpment that has stood firm for millennia against the relentless scrape of glaciers, wind, and rain. To the Māori, this long ridge is the supine shape of the giant Te Mata, who died for love. Tricked by his lover's family into trying to swallow the peak, he choked, died, and became the mountain.

The hike was recommended by our Napier B&B hosts, Tom and Esther, though with their New Zealand accents I thought they were telling me to climb *Tomato* Peak. They said it was the most popular hike in the area. Indeed, a view so magnificent is meant to be shared, and so, after steeling my nerves for a vertigo-inducing walk, puffing my way up to the very top, I was not totally surprised to see lots of folks up there who had taken the shorter route — from the summit parking lot.

More sobering, however, was the realization that this awesome rolling grassland, which looks so much like the wild steppes of Mongolia, is not at all natural. It is man-made, constructed landscape. These hills were once forested. But, when settlers "bought" land in the 1800s — either through sales enforced over the objections of the Māori tribal leaders or expropriated outright by the Crown — they cleared the trees

The view from Te Mata Peak. The parking lot is next to the tree.

and brush and replaced it with pasture for sheep farming, and later, for cattle. Here's a close-up (below) from the lower center-right of the photo above:

Close-up of the lower-middle section of the photo above: dots are sheep and cows.

You can see not only the black dots of cattle and the white dots of sheep, but also the lines on the landscape that make it look like a topographical map. Those are well-worn animal tracks. In the second half of the 1800s and early 1900s, roughly 50% of the entire surface of New Zealand was cleared of trees and converted to grassland by British settlers, most of it for sheep — for wool to feed England's ravenous textile mills. The Wellington Te Papa Museum illustrates the drastic impact of land conversion on New Zealand's native forest in three maps.

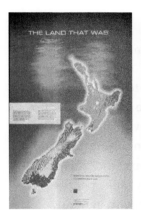

Left: 1200 (before arrival of Te Māori): 85% natural forest. Center: 1840: 600 years of Māori settlement reduced the natural forest cover to 55%. Right: Today: after 180 years of European settlement, only 25% of natural forest cover remains. (My photos from the Wellington Te Papa Museum)

This change was not easy on the land. The Wellington Te Papa Museum displays excerpts from a book written by a sheep farmer, George Guthrie-Smith, who bought land in the 1880s. Forty years later, he wrote a book, *Tutira: The Story of a New Zealand Sheep Station*, in which he made prescient and grim predictions about New Zealand's natural environment. He came to see the breaking of the land as an act of violence: "It is no exaggeration to say that the surface had to be stamped, hammered, hauled, murdered into grass." He also saw that, once converted, the grass would sometimes fail to hold the soil in place, leading to landslips and erosion after heavy rains. I saw some of these ugly land slips myself on the pastured hills near Te Mata. They looked as if some malicious being had torn great strips from the green skin of the supine giant.

However, Te Mata is also symbolic of the growing conservation awareness of New Zealanders. Much of the area around the peak is now a protected park. On my hike, I noticed whole hillsides being replanted with native seedlings. According to the Te Mata Park website:

> As a memorial to their father, John Chambers' sons gifted a 242 acre (99 hectare) reserve on the upper Havelock North hills, including Te Mata Peak, to the people of Hawke's Bay in perpetuity. A charitable trust was set up for the benefit of all citizens of the provincial district of Hawke's Bay with the intention of maintaining the land as a recreational reserve. This generous and forward-thinking gift has benefitted not only the people of Hawke's Bay, but the New Zealand public in general...

After a bit more digging online, I discovered that John Chambers came to Hawke's Bay in 1854. He bought and leased vast tracts of land to clear for sheep farming, and he wanted the land around Te Mata. According to his biography in *The Encyclopedia of New Zealand* (teara.govt.nz), "Chambers had also been squatting on the west bank of the Tukituki River, on the Te Mata block, an area still in Māori hands; the authorities acquiesced in this illegal occupation for fear of losing a valuable settler..."

To be blunt about it: Chambers stole Te Mata from the Māori tribe that owned it, and the government turned a blind eye. Chambers went on to amass and clear over 18,000 acres for sheep farming, land for which he paid a "minimal price." He also pioneered methods of preserving meat to ship overseas, and though he was not the one to perfect the process, he played a big role in founding Hawke's Bay's meat-freezing trade.

New Zealand, remember, was too far away from the rest of the world to export its meat. Freezer ships breathed new life into New Zealand sheep farming, which previously could only export wool. Global demand for wool was waning, but the market for meat was booming. Thus, the new freezer technology buoyed New Zealand's economy for many decades to come. By 1970, there were 70 million sheep in New Zealand. That's about 20 sheep per person! Enough for each resident to have their own flock.

New Zealand lamb has become a global premium brand, and restaurants always point it out when the lamb on their menu comes from New Zealand. Today, the country is still the second-largest exporter of lamb in the world, after Australia.

Nevertheless, as synthetics gradually replaced wool in the 1960s, the shift hit New Zealand sheep farmers hard. These days, it costs a farmer almost as much to shear a sheep as the price of the fleece on the market. The world has passed peak sheep. In 2023, there are only 26 million sheep in New Zealand: the lowest number in 170 years. According to a recent *Guardian* article, many sheep farmers are getting out of the business. They are selling their land for — guess what? Replanting forests for carbon credits. (See "New Zealand falls out of love with sheep farming as lucrative pine forests spread," *The Guardian*, June 30, 2023.)

The New Zealand government is taking seriously its net-zero emission targets. Methane from sheep and cows makes up 50% of the nation's greenhouse gases, and replanting farmland with fast-growing pine trees has become a key part of their strategy. Many global companies are also buying up New Zealand farmland to plant trees for carbon credits. As a result, says the *Guardian* article, New Zealand's sheep farmers are getting six times as much from selling their land for reforesting than for agricultural use.

There is a crazy irony to all this, isn't there? Early European settlers "murdered" the land to make their fortunes literally off the backs of sheep. A hundred and seventy years later, sheep are on the way out, and farmers are profiting from turning the land back into forest. Of course, it is not quite so tidy. A good number of those fast-growing pines in the hills above Hawke's Bay got flooded out by Cyclone Gabrielle in early 2023. They came crashing down the rivers, wiping out bridges, infrastructure, and houses in their way — destruction we had witnessed ourselves on our drive into Napier. In addition, these fast-growing pines are not native; like any invasive species, they can spread into the remaining natural forests, where, unchecked, they will choke out the native trees and take over the landscape. A tree farm is not the same as a natural forest.

It turns out you can't simply replant to repent for your sins.

Chapter 10

In Wellington: New Zealand's Treasure Box

Lambdon Quay, in the heart of Wellington, is an odd name for a street that is 250 meters (800 feet) from the water's edge. A quay is a dock area. It's supposed to be on the shoreline. But in 1855 a massive earthquake uplifted the land beneath the new capital city by 1.5 meters (5 feet) and left the quay high and dry. The newly emerged land immediately became prime real estate, and once they got the idea, city planners and developers carried on, reclaiming more and more land from the sea in the subsequent century by infilling the shallows.

Right on the water's edge today, built on newly reclaimed land, is the Museum of New Zealand Te Papa Tongarewa. *Te Papa* means "Treasure Box" in te reo Māori. It's not just the land beneath the museum that has been reclaimed; the art, the history, and the *narrative* have also been reclaimed. Previously, this official custodian of New Zealand's past was known as the Colonial Museum. But Te Papa is something new and unique: a *de-colonizing* museum.

In countries with a colonial past, museums usually tell the nation's history from the perspective of the dominant culture as "us" and the indigenous peoples as "them." Te Papa tells the story of Te Māori and the story of Pākehā (European settlers and their descendants) as the story of "us, together." In this way it lives up to the founding document of New Zealand, the Treaty of Waitangi, as a partnership between two peoples.

The treaty was violated hundreds of times by the colonists since signing. But in the mid-1970s, in response to Māori protests about the continuing takeover of their lands (including a 1975 Gandhi-style protest march to Wellington of over 1100 kilometers (700 miles), led by the indomitable 79-year-old

Whina Cooper), the New Zealand government agreed to set up a tribunal. The Waitangi Tribunal has since addressed over 2000 claims, and recommended many changes that have set the government back on a path to genuine partnership. The original Waitangi Treaty is on display at Te Papa, in a prominent place of honor on the main floor.

As an author and storyteller, one of the reasons museums fascinate me is because I see them as the way a society tells the story *of* itself *to* itself. If the "artifacts" of a minority indigenous community are shoved into cases in a back room, that says something about their place in the dominant culture's narrative. Even if the artifacts are prominently displayed, if they are nevertheless treated like exhibits of ancient Egyptians or other exotic "dead" peoples, that framing tells you something important. To turn another's culture into a collection of objects that can be defined and displayed is rather like capturing a butterfly and sticking a pin through it. Preserved as part of a collection, it has no more life.

I had first been sensitized to this the previous year at a museum in northern Norway that was run by the indigenous Sámi community. Their most prominent exhibit was a ritual drum which had been returned to the Sámi people by the government of Denmark in 2022. To the Sámi, a ritual drum is not an artifact; it is a "non-human person" with a spirit and will of its own. Having the drum returned was like having an ancestor brought home. The drum was given its own special room, and could not be photographed. It was treated more like an honored guest than an object. It shocked me to suddenly realize that museums all over the world hold "artifacts" in their collections that have different and deeper meanings for the living communities that they were taken from.

The most amazing example of the shift of narrative in Te Papa is the exhibition of the historic Māori gathering place, Te Hau ki Tūranga, of the Rongowhakaata *iwi* (tribe). The structure dominates the main display room of the Māori history section. For Māori tribes, these buildings function as a combination of church, museum, memorial, town hall, and community center all under one roof. In 1867, this exact building was simply confiscated by the government. Without asking for the consent of the iwi, it was dismantled, taken from tribal land to Wellington, and then reassembled inside the Colonial Museum. It sat there on display for more than 100 years, as an *example* of a Te Hau ki Tūranga.

Can you imagine a group of outsiders coming into your hometown, ripping apart the main church, and carting the pieces off to put it in their museum?

Only in 2012 was ownership of the building returned to the Rongowhakaata tribe. They have agreed to let Te Papa continue to display their building, but also to tell the horrific story of how it was taken. Importantly, the building's status as a sacred space has been restored. One cannot walk inside, and no photographs are allowed. *That* is a new narrative of mutual respect and collaboration that also owns the wrongs of the past.

Te Hau ki Tūranga of the Rongowhakaata tribe, as installed at Te Papa. (My photo is of a *photo* of the Te Hau ki Tūranga next to the display that explains its story.)

The museum also features an impressive temporary exhibit dedicated to the *waka*, the Maori canoe, and specifically to the large canoes that were reconstructed for a massive ceremony in 2020 to commemorate the 180th anniversary of the Waitangi Treaty. These were huge boats, holding as many as 50 paddlers, decorated with intricate carvings and ornamented with feathers. Each tribal group built and paddled their community's canoe to the ceremony at Waitangi. The Prime Minister at the time, Jacinda Ardern, also took part. Photos of her rowing a Māori canoe filled with young New Zealanders (part of the museum's display) symbolized her government's commitment to a future in which settler and Māori communities pulled together. After all, they *are* all in the same boat.

From the *waka* (canoe) exhibit in Te Papa Museum, Wellington

I was also struck by the portion of the museum dedicated to natural history, and not just because the placards were in both English and te reo Māori. (Te reo Māori was only made an official language of New Zealand in 1987.) As well as two languages, the museum provided two complementary *narratives*. For example, there was a prominent exhibit titled "Awesome Forces" on earthquakes and volcanic eruptions. Side by side with the science, the museum tells the origin story of

Rūaumoko, the Māori god of earthquakes and volcanoes I had recently learned about in Taupō.

According to Māori tradition, earthquakes are caused by the god Rūaumoko (or Rūamoko), the son of Ranginui (the Sky) and his wife Papatūānuku (the Earth). Rangi had been separated from Papatūānuku, and his tears had flooded the land. Their sons resolved to turn their mother's face downwards, so that she and Rangi should not constantly see one another's sorrow and grieve more. When Papatūānuku was turned over, Rūaumoko was still at her breast, and was carried to the world below. To keep him warm there, he was given fire. He is the god of earthquakes and volcanoes, and the rumblings that disturb the land are made by him as he walks about.

A trail of Rūaumoko's footsteps winds through the geological explanations of tectonic forces and subterranean magma reservoirs. I appreciated how seamlessly the two narratives of myth and science were woven together in the exhibit hall — not as if one was true and the other false, but rather, that these are two ways of connecting with the reality of these mighty and terrifying forces far beneath our feet.

The museum also had a special area for children which, at the time of our visit, was devoted to events and activities celebrating Matariki, the Māori New Year. This is a time of year when tribal communities gather to remember their ancestors, something like the Mexican "Day of the Dead." In 2022 Matariki became an official national holiday in New Zealand. It is the first public holiday that marks a Māori holiday. Traditionally, Māori take two weeks to gather and celebrate at this time of year, which varies according to the lunar calendar. A nationwide two-week school semester break now takes place aligned with these dates.

In the run-up to Matariki, an entire outside wall of the museum had been turned into a dazzling Matariki night-light show, combining the design work of traditional Māori artists with modern light-projection techniques. Illuminated posters next to the wall explained the legend of Matariki, also known as the constellation of the Pleiades, and the meaning of each star as a specific celestial divinity from Māori mythology. The museum events and other celebrations were not simply for tribal children, but were framed inclusively for every child, and portrayed as part of their identity as New Zealanders.

Matariki motifs projected onto the exterior walls of Te Papa Museum

From the museum website:

Matariki is the star cluster most commonly known across the world as Pleiades ... Around the world there are many names for this group of stars. In Japan, it is called Subaru, which means 'to come together'. In China it is Mao, the hairy head of the white tiger, and in India it is known as Krittika. In Greek mythology they are known as the seven sisters, and in Norse mythology the Vikings knew them as Freyja's hens ... For many cultures, these stars are connected to celebration, planting, harvesting, weather, and life. For Māori, the rising of Matariki signals te Mātahi o te Tau, the Māori New Year. The appearance of Matariki in the morning sky is a sign for people to gather, to honour the dead, celebrate the present, and plan for the future.

As well as designating Matakiri a national holiday over a long weekend, the government also encourages all New Zealanders to use this special time to gather as families and to: "Remember the past, honour the dead, celebrate the present, and plan for the future."

Truly, this is a blueprint for de-colonizing that countries everywhere could well adopt.

Part Two

South Island

Chapter 11

Abel Tasman National Park: Gold Beaches, Emerald Forests, Sapphire Seas

There's a magical little corner of New Zealand that's off the radar of most foreign visitors: the north coast of the South Island. It's just a few hours by car from where the ferry crosses the Cook Strait and disgorges passengers arriving from Wellington on the North Island. Most travelers take the main highway southeast to Christchurch. But Teresa and I turned west and followed the winding coast road past the towns of Nelson and Richmond towards the remote Abel Tasman National Park.

Only about 18,000 people inhabit the coastal areas on either side of the park: Tasman Bay to the south, and the evocatively named Golden Bay to the north. In summer, the beaches along these bays are prime destinations for New Zealanders vacationing by tent or RV. Hotel accommodation is scarce and relatively expensive, but in mid-July — wintertime — the region is pretty quiet, even though various microclimates make it the warmest part of the cold South Island.

We had no problem booking a beachfront hotel, nor getting a table at one of the three open restaurants in the village of Kaiterikeri where we stayed (see page C10). Most crucially, it was easy for me to book a last-minute passage the following morning on a boat to Abel Tasman Park.

Hiking in this national park and marine reserve was at the top of my must-do list for the region. A three-day-long wilderness trail runs through Abel Tasman Park, but there are no access roads for hikers. Small passenger ferries, however, accommodate day-trippers, allowing them to land on six of the beaches where the park coast intersects with the trail. The boat drops you off at one wilderness beach and picks you up, hours later, at another. As the Kiwis say, it's "sweet as."

And so, leaving Teresa in her own "sweet as" happy place (balcony view of the beach) that morning, I left Kaiterikeri's golden beach for the emerald greens of the park's interior. Out of about 20 passengers, I was the only one to disembark at my particular stop. The lone crew member lowered the electronic gangplank as we motored towards the empty beach.

"Jump," he told me.

Beach-to-beach boat taxi for Abel Tasman day-trippers

I leapt over the last wave, landing on soft sand, my boots still dry. A minute later, the boat was gone and I was all alone. I would not pass half a dozen hikers on the trail all day.

Immersed in this wild green world, I quickly noticed just how different the forest here was from anything I'd experienced in the northern hemisphere. It felt primeval — Jurassic, even. I realized this was due to the giant fern trees. They were shaped like palms, but with huge fern branches spread out at the top. Looking straight up from the trunk of one, the lattice-like patterns looked like a great, green, embroidered umbrella, diffusing the sunlight to the forest floor (see page C11).

The next thing I noticed was the music. The forest was filled with birdsong. And not your average, chirpy-chirp, tweety-tweet stuff. Bell-birds and tūi were going at it as if Abel Tasman was having a bell-ringing and flute-tooting competition at the same time. I'd heard a lot of tūi now that we were a month into our travels in New Zealand. But usually I'd heard these black birds with the white "parson's collar" throat feathers in city parks. Here in the wild forest, they fully let loose. Unlike most birds with a signature cheep or trill, the tūi has an incredible range and variety. The bird is a mimic and can reproduce everything from telephones to farm machinery. Four or five birds within earshot were improvising their little hearts out. Sometimes they would seem to sing in response to each other. Were they conversing, or showing off? I felt like I was in the middle of a free-flowing, forest-wide, bird-jazz jam session.

One of the strangest things about some of the birds in New Zealand is their lack of wariness towards humans. Tiny pīwakaka flew back and forth in front of me as I hiked, hovering like miniature drones to get a better look. They have a long, white fantail which they twist side to side as they fly, making them highly maneuverable. They would follow me for five or ten minutes at a stretch, as if watching me was the most interesting part of their day.

Every time I sat down to rest at a bench or convenient picnic table, a flightless brown weka bird would soon pop out of the underbrush and walk right up to me. One of them even pecked curiously at my boot! I soon realized these hen-sized birds had each claimed an individual territory around hiker rest-stops. They were not simply curious. They were mooching. I confess to a serious breach of judgment: I gave one weka a few lumps of a banana I was eating. I should know better than to feed the birds. But these weka... they are so adorable, so good at wheedling. It was too hard for me to resist.

Abel Tasman Park: left: fern trees; right: wheedling weka

Sadly, the one bird that eluded me was the kākā — a large, endangered parrot with russet-red-brown feathers. I had seen photos and read about it at the Wellington Te Papa Museum, and knew there was a project to restore them in Abel Tasman Park, with several dozen pairs released into the park over the past few years.

The track wound through dense forest, wetland boardwalks, along empty gold-sand beaches — not too hilly, but twisty and turny enough to keep the mind focused and the old gams working. I stepped in and out of valleys where the temperature and light shifted and suddenly the vegetation was markedly different. These pockets were too small to be considered microclimates. Were they *nano*climates? Black moss covered some trees in these zones. At first it looked as if they'd been burned. I had to touch the spongy stuff to be sure it was real.

From one beach, I noticed a stand of dead conifer trees on a hillside. A nearby plaque explained that these were the infamous "wilding pines" that had been deliberately killed, because they were invasive. Seeds were blowing in from a nearby forestry plantation. The invaders grew quickly, crowding out native trees. Left unchecked, they would take over the whole park.

There is now a concerted effort in Abel Tasman and many other parts of the country to stem the invasion by killing wilding pines with powerful herbicides and then letting them decompose in place. Even way out here in the wilderness, humankind's attempts to "manage" nature and extract a profit were having unintended and disastrous consequences.

Here and there in the forest, Māori elements would appear — ornamentation on bridges, or a life-sized, carved vermillion statue of an ancestor spirit in a clearing. These reminded me that for Te Māori, the forest was not simply a resource or recreation space. Special places in the park are woven into the mythology and history of their people, making them sacred (see page C11).

Teresa and I visited one such sacred place the following day. Just north of Abel Tasman, Te Waikoropupū is where the largest cold-water spring south of the Equator gushes to the surface, the color of an aquamarine gemstone. It produces some of the purest, clearest water in the world. In ages past, these waters were sacred to the Māori iwi who lived nearby. Then, in the 1850s, a European prospector discovered gold in a nearby river and the rush was on. By the early 1860s the forest surrounding Te Waikoropupū had been burned to the ground and the land cleared for prospecting. Water races were built to carry water from the spring's creeks for sluicing crushed rocks to aid in the search for gold.

But gold was never found in this particular valley. The prospectors eventually moved on, leaving behind a wasteland. A hundred and fifty years later, the forest has regrown, and the settler family that inherited the land has donated it back to the Department of Conservation, in collaboration with the local iwi.

Teresa and I were moved by the carved gateway and placards explaining both the purity of the waters and the Māori mythology of the place. One reads:

In Māori tradition the Springs are waiora, the purest form of water which is the wairua (spiritual) and the physical source of life. The Springs provide water for healing, and in the past were a place of ceremonial blessings at times of birth and death and the leaving and returning of travellers.

Visitors today are prohibited from touching the pools where the springs flow, and only the local tribe members are allowed to take and use its waters. The spring has not simply been restored. It has been re-sacralized.

Back in Abel Tasman Park, my trek was nearing its end. I reached the last beach for my pickup 45 minutes early, so I decided to explore the trail ahead a little further, and then double back. Just ten minutes later I heard a kerfuffle of wings above me. I looked up and saw that I had startled a large reddish-brown bird with a short, curved beak: a kākā! The big parrot landed on another branch nearby. It was impossible to photograph him high in the trees. I could only watch him, my neck craning, my heart filled with hope for his kind, and with gratitude for the folks who dedicate their time and effort to restoring New Zealand's natural heritage.

Chapter 12

Pancake Rocks: The Stacks
That Stump the Scientists

The west coast of the South Island is truly wild. So wild in fact that no more than 30,000 hardy souls live along the whole stretch of it. One can't actually drive it all. There are big chunks where the shoreline is so rugged and broken by mountains and cliffs, rivers and fjords, that there's no point even trying to put a road through, and so the route that travels the length of the west coast detours well inland in three places. The rewards, however, for riding this road-less-traveled is that one gets to experience some of the unique wonders of the country that the majority of tourists miss: the twin glaciers of Fox and Franz Josef that come right down into the rainforest; secluded glacial lakes; imposing vertical cliffs that early peoples could only traverse by climbing woven grass ropes; and the historic gold-mining town of Hokitika (setting of the New Zealand bestseller and miniseries *The Luminaries*).

But the strangest highlight of the west coast is the geological freak show known as Pancake Rocks. The name of the place conveys the idea easily enough: rock formations along the coast that are in layers, like, duh, big stacks of pancakes. Teresa and I wandered from the car park through a flax-bush forest to the headland at Dolomite Point, ready to be mildly amused by the phenomenon. We were unprepared for the truly otherworldly grandeur of it all (see page C12). To name all this magnificence after pancakes is like labeling the Grand Canyon "Deep Valley," or calling Mitre Peak "Hat Mountain," or the Florida Everglades "The Big Wet Lawn."

The statue of a gold miner in Hokitika points the way for a young backpacker —
a new breed of treasure hunter.

I find the original Māori names for geological features are
often much more evocative than the names bestowed on them
by early European explorers (who liked to name landmarks after
other white men). Māori names are often derived from myths of
the gods who created New Zealand, whose likenesses turned
to stone to make mountains, or whose digging sticks furrowed
vast valleys. But in this case, the Māori name for Pancake Rocks,
Punakāiki, is simply a phonetic approximation of the English
word "pancake." Though the Māori iwi had seasonal camps
in the area, it was not settled, and this impressive geological
formation never inherited a myth of its own.

To my twenty-first-century eyes, the formations actually looked as if some divine computer programmer had picked the world's most dramatic limestone cliff coastline, and then copied it on a landscape-scale 3-D printer. Okay, I realize, now that I've written it, that "3-D Printer Rocks" is perhaps no improvement on breakfast carbs.

What I find most intriguing about these cliffs is that, according to one of the placards along the Pancake Rocks walkway, scientists don't know exactly what caused the rocks to form like this. How cool is that? A geological phenomenon that has stumped science!

Oh sure, they have a name for the phenomenon: *stylobedding*. And the main geological forces are clear enough: the limestone cliffs were formed around 30 million years ago, when layers of dead corals and shells accumulated on what was once a seabed, and then calcified into limestone and dolomite, which are as hard as concrete. As the land rose in subsequent geological eras, wind and tide washed away the silty sediments between the calcified layers, *yada yada yada*, creating the unique, stack-like appearance. But the "yada-yada-yada" part glosses over why hundreds of distinct layers formed at Punakāiki (and a few other places around the world), but not on the vast majority of limestone beach-cliffs on the planet. What specific conditions created the layers?

I think it's great that geologists are still working on that one. Science is supposed to be a process of discovery, experimentation, and debate. So it's lovely to run into something so magnificent that remains a mystery.

Chapter 13

Up the Forked Tongue of Franz Josef Glacier

One of the must-do destinations for me on New Zealand's remote west coast was Franz Josef Glacier. Of the 2900 glaciers in New Zealand, Franz Josef is one of the largest, 12 kilometers (7.5 miles) at present, and one of only three that flow down to the level of the rainforest. So, on the day we arrived at the eponymous village of Franz Josef, you can imagine how I felt to discover the sky was overcast; rain and fog was forecast. We would see nothing. Yes, I was downcast.

Teresa happily hunkered down in our hotel room. We were spending three days in this teeny-tiny settlement next to the glacier mostly for me. Glaciers fascinate me, and the prospect of seeing Franz Josef up close compelled me out the door to hike to the nearest lookout, never mind the light rain. You can guess what I saw at the viewpoint: a vast gravel riverbed with a wall of dense cloud just beyond it. This was the moraine of the glacier, which over the past 150 years has retreated about 3 kilometers (2 miles) up the valley. Today it was invisible. A hundred and fifty years ago, according to a placard at the lookout, from this spot the glacier flowed far into the valley, a colossal river, a Ganges of ice.

I also discovered that the hiking route up the moraine to the edge of the current glacier was permanently closed. Previously, hikers could walk right up and put their hand on the tip of the glacier's frozen tongue. But just a few years ago, the river changed course. Now the water flows down from the glacier right over the old path. There is no longer a safe trail up the riverbed, which can flood rapidly and without warning. These days, only two steep, strenuous, slippery-when-wet hikes much higher up the hillsides can get adventurous trampers to a decent view of the ice. The hikes take five to eight hours round trip, and I didn't have the nerve to try them, especially in rainy weather. I looked at the gray gravel, the gray sky, and scowled.

Left: Franz Josef Glacier in the 1870s. Right: The same viewpoint today. What remains of the glacier is hiding in the mist.

Instead of simply sulking, the next day I signed up for a kayak trip on nearby Lake Mapourika. The trip website advertised glacier views from the lake. But only when the sky is clear, and alas, the rain persisted. The paddling was still well worth it, though, especially for what I learned about the glacier from the lead guide, a Canadian expat named Dale. Dale explained that Franz Josef is only one of three temperate glaciers in the southern hemisphere. The rest melted away long ago. It's actually most unusual to have a glacier flow right down to the level of a rainforest. This happens because of a unique combination of climate and geology. Prevailing winds blow hot air from Australia east over the cool Tasman Sea, picking up moisture. When the wet wind hits the coast of New Zealand it is forced up the side of the Southern Alps, creating rain, and higher up, snow. At the foot of the mountains, in the rainforest, about 500–800 centimeters (200–300 inches) of rain falls each year on average; up in the glaciers, it's more like 1500 centimeters (600 inches), precipitating as ice and snow, feeding and refilling the icefields at the source of the glaciers.

According to Dale, between 1983 and 2008 while most of the world's glaciers were retreating due to climate change, Franz Josef actually *grew larger*. It gained back nearly half the ice it had lost over the previous century. Since then, the ice has shrunk dramatically again.

Later that day, Teresa and I took a drive out towards the next glacier down the road. Fox Glacier is just 30 kilometers away (less than 20 miles), and also flows through the rainforest. From the distant viewpoint, despite the clouds, we got a great view of it. My photo (below) is from several miles away, but it gives a great perspective on the size of these ice behemoths.

Fox Glacier

The viewpoint contained an elaborate artwork of a giant Māori canoe, representative of the Māori myth about the mountain range that runs along the center of the South Island: Te Wahipounamu was formed when the four sons of Ranginui, the Sky Father, descended from the heavens in a sea canoe and set out on a voyage to visit their mother, Papatūānuku, the Earth Mother. During this voyage their canoe hit a reef, and icy wind caused the canoe to capsize. The brothers scrambled to the top of the canoe to escape the water, but they froze into stone. The canoe became the South Island, and the brothers turned into the tall mountains that dominate the mountain ridge that runs up the center of the island.

Our third and final day, I got up early for a hike to another Fox Glacier lookout — never mind the thick mist. I was resigned to missing Franz Josef. But by noon the mist had cleared, revealing a pure blue sky. I raced back to our hotel. There was only one remaining option for us getting a close-up view of a glacier.

"Hey sweetheart, how about a helicopter ride?" I said to my bride when I returned, shocking the pants off her. I'm not usually prone to splurges, and it would cost us $200 (US) each for the 25-minute round trip, including a brief touchdown at the top of the glacier. My obsessive math-calculator brain kicked in: that would be $8 per minute apiece. Suddenly, that number sounded quite reasonable, as every second of the flight was sure to be spectacular.

"Absolutely! When shall we go?" she replied with great aplomb, as if she had been sitting around waiting for such an invitation all afternoon. Though sometimes Teresa gets a bit of vertigo — on high bridges, etc. — she seemed quite nonchalant about this little jaunt.

"Well, we have to leave right now..."

An hour later Teresa and I were strapped into our seats in a plexiglass dome, the rotors whirling overhead. We lifted off — one pilot, five passengers — and soared towards the glacier, hugging the high, green walls of the valley, our delicate bubble swaying gently from side to side with each adjustment of our course. In minutes we had Franz Josef in sight, and for the first time I could see its massive, forked tongue, mineral blue, rough and jagged at the edge (see page C13).

We flew right over top of the tongue and up over the icefield that had given birth to the glacier thousands of years ago. The snow was brilliant white, newly fallen from the previous days' precipitation. I had a side window seat, and so, on the banked turns, I was basically looking straight down into the crevasses. Looking behind me, I could see clear down the valley to the Tasman Sea.

Graceful as a bee alighting on a flower, our pilot set the helicopter down on a flat space of hard-packed snow. He hopped out, and set us free, but told us not to go too far; we could not tell exactly where the snow curved off the edge of our little perch. We staggered around a bit, disoriented by the thin air and sheer exhilaration of being right up here in this bright ice palace in the sky, among the frozen brother-gods of legend. The pilot, calmly and in turn, took each of our cameras and got us to pose. He was good. We look so poised, so relaxed in our photos. Inside, I felt delirious.

Tim and Teresa, looking too cool on top of Franz Josef Glacier

"Nice job you've got," I told him. "You get to make people crazy-happy every day."

"Yeah," the pilot drawled, looking around from the peaks to the ocean at the end of the valley. "This is my office."

As we climbed on board, I offered Teresa my window seat for the flight back down Franz Josef. She looked at me like I was nuts.

"No!"

"But you'll see so much more."

"I doubt it. I had my eyes closed almost the whole way up!"

Chapter 14

Queenstown: Chic Town

Queenstown is situated on the shores of a stunning glacial lake surrounded by snow-frosted mountains. The town is also the foodie capital of New Zealand's South Island. And there are 75 independent vineyards within 20 kilometers (12 miles). It's as if the divine forces of the universe handcrafted this place to perfectly match Teresa's proclivities.

"*This* is where we are going to splurge," she informed me in advance of our trip. "In Queenstown, we are going to *blow the wad!*"

And why not? Why save it for our children's inheritance when before us lay a land of boutique luxury hotels and gourmet bistros surrounded by glittering peaks?

After two weeks in the remote north and west coasts of the South Island, Teresa and I were dazzled by the sights and sounds of the big city (population 15,800). Teresa booked us into the trendiest restaurants in town, which served local delicacies like blue cod and kumara (a kind of sweet potato). She also picked out the fanciest cocktail bars for us to hit, including Eichardt's Bar, snuggled into the oldest hotel in Queenstown, and built by the very man who founded the town.

Queenstown got its start in the 1860s when a Māori farmhand, Jack Tewa, found gold on the land of his employer, the first sheep rancher to settle in the region, William Gilbert Rees. Rees's farm covered the area that became Queenstown. The government requisitioned half his land for £10,000 to make room for the gold-boom development. Apparently, the government never noticed the place had been used seasonally by Māori tribes for hundreds of years previously — there was no recompense for them!

Rees built the first hotel (now Eichardt's) and set up a shipping business importing supplies for the miners. Today he is considered the founder of Queenstown. His statue (below) stands by the waterfront, next to what was once his hotel.

A girl scampered up the memorial statue of Rees in central Queenstown for a better view. Off camera, the child's parents are yelling at her to get down from there, and she is totally ignoring them.

When the gold boom ended, Queenstown found a second life in tourism, which sustains the town to this day. In the 1950s, a ski run was constructed on a nearby peak. This gave Queenstown *two* tourist seasons, so it's basically packed all year round.

Teresa booked us for five nights at the Hulbert House Hotel, a luxury boutique B&B in an old house that was first owned by Horatio Nelson Firth. Firth was the "receiver" of prospectors' gold on behalf of a bank during the gold-rush years. Unfortunately, Mr. Firth made a habit of pocketing some of the gold for himself, and got caught. He was sent to prison for five years, leaving his wife Mary and their children to fend for themselves. The resourceful Mrs. Firth opened a hotel, which has stayed in business ever since.

It's now owned by a Japanese artist who has redecorated with extravagantly bold patterns and colors — twilight indigo and jungle green — and maintains Mrs. Firth's high standards. When they showed us to our room, Teresa experienced some sort of transfiguration experience, a moment of sheer joy. It was all she could do not to burst into tears.

"I *never* want to leave this room!" she announced.

Teresa in her natural habitat

What we both loved about Hulbert House were the staff members, who came from all over to work here: England, the United States, Uruguay, Japan, even Australia. They seemed to be having the time of their lives, skiing before shifts, hiking on days off, and enjoying the nightlife. Their *joie de vivre* was part of what made the place so special. I even heard one of the staff singing to herself while cleaning the toilets!

The excursion Teresa was most looking forward to was the boat ride along Lake Wakatipu in the steamship TSS *Earnslaw*. Built by the company that made the *Titanic*, it was launched onto the lake in 1912 (the very year the *Titanic* sank). The ship used to haul supplies for miners and farmers in from Kingston, the town at the southern tip of the lake, which by then was connected to the railway. Saved from the scrapheap in the 1950s, the TSS *Earnslaw* was refurbished as a tourist cruise ship and made more glamorous, with wood-panel interiors and a wine bar (see page C15).

On board, one can sit in the upper lounge, sipping a glass of Otago Valley Pinot Noir and listening to the piano player while watching the white-capped mountains slide by in a stately procession. Or one can head below to explore the antique engine room, and gaze out the portholes to watch the mountains at sea level. And of course, one can pose for the camera on the bow, taking turns with other tourists for a *Titanic* "king of the world" photo op. We did it all.

Now, I must clarify that Teresa also wanted to stay in Queenstown for several days because she knew it would be ideal for her hiker-hubby; the hills around Queenstown are a trekker's paradise. In fact, just a ten-minute walk from our door I found myself at the trailhead of the hike to Queenstown Peak, with spectacular views of the lake, the town, and higher up, 360-degree views of the mountains (see page C14).

The climb passed through a dense and dark pine forest. A sign above the treeline told the distressing story of these trees — New Zealand's notorious "wilding pines" — and the efforts to keep them from overtaking the native vegetation in this fragile region. The pines are introduced species from North America, white pine and lodgepole mostly. They have no natural enemies in New Zealand, and so spread like weeds. They also suck up a lot of groundwater, lowering the water table. This can have devastating consequences in drier areas, such as the nearby Otago vineyards. According to the www.wildingpines.nz website, over a quarter of New Zealand's land is in danger of being overrun by this menace.

Originally brought to New Zealand for timber plantations, the trees were also used by the government in a misguided effort to stem erosion on mountain hillsides. Helicopters would scatter seeds by the millions. But instead of preventing erosion, the government unleashed a plague. Now, efforts to remove the trees are costly, dangerous, and complicated. Apparently, deforestation goes against New Zealand's climate-change policies, so one part of the government requires another part to pay a *fine* for destroying invasive pines!

One afternoon Teresa and I drove out to the nearby Otago vineyards for wine tasting. At Kinross Winery we sampled the product of five local winemakers at one go. What was most interesting to us is that the famous Otago Valley Pinot Noirs have a distinctive, earthy bouquet. *Umami* is the technical wine-tasting term for it. One could kindly describe it as "mushroomy." But honestly, to me, the wines smelled ever so faintly of sewer pipes. More like, *Ew-mammie!* That put me off the taste somewhat. But Teresa insisted the wines were complex and intriguing once one gets them past the nose.

Clearly, New Zealanders agree, because the boutique winemakers of Otago sell out their vintages year after year. The friendly woman presiding over our tasting told us it's almost impossible to get an older vintage of the local wines because demand is so high, they're all gone after a year or two. Well, good for them! We bought a few bottles of Pinot Noir, and though *umami*-like gases continued to waft from my glass, I persisted until I actually got past the initial stink and discovered mineral and dark fruit flavors underneath that really were unique. *Yum-Mammie!*

On our last day in Queenstown, we took a drive to the far end of Lake Wakatipu, past the sheep farms of Glenorchy and along a dirt road called Paradise Drive. This wild country was most famously used for scenes from the *Lord of the Rings* movies that called for vast mountain panoramas. Not even the sheep have made it this far into the wilderness. We drove until the very end of the road, exhilarated by the wild green forests and the granite, white-capped peaks that emerged and receded from the clouds, like lurking giants.

All too suddenly, after five glorious days, it was time for us to leave Queenstown. The staff at Hulbert House Hotel gave us warm hugs goodbye and wished us well on our journey to Milford Sound. There were tears, the wringing of hands, attempts to bargain and plead with the universe, and so much wailing as we drove off... Teresa was sad to leave, too.

Chapter 15

A Prayer for Milford Sound

The "Eighth Wonder of the World," Rudyard Kipling called it. For over 140 years, Milford Sound has epitomized remote, pristine, awe-inspiring nature. Conjure an image of New Zealand — a mist-shrouded mountain rising straight up from the sea — and chances are you are recalling a photo or poster you once saw of Milford Sound. We were no different. Teresa and I built our entire trip to New Zealand around our visit to Milford Sound. Yet, as we departed Queenstown for the four-and-a-half-hour drive to the Fiordland, mingled with the excitement was a bit of fear. There was snow in the forecast, and the authorities had already announced the high mountain road — the only road into the fjord — was going to close at 4:30 that afternoon. (Technically, Milford is a *fjord*, not a *sound*, while Fiordland Park uses the less common spelling of *fjord*).

Online, we learned that snow chains were required for the tires of all cars driving that road in winter. We gulped, but found a service station in Te Anau that rented chains. Te Anau is the last town on the road before one reaches Milford Sound, another two hours further into the wilderness. The friendly woman behind the station counter told us, *yeah-nah*, our spiffy Polestar had wheels that could not, in fact, be fitted with chains without damaging them. But no worries, she said with a bright smile, no need for chains; we were well ahead of the storm.

I gulped again and shook off my anxiety. I'm a *Canadian* for God's sake, I reminded myself. I don't need no stinkin' chains.

So, back in the Polestar, with the weather sunny-cloudy as we entered the Fiordland National Park. The fjords dominate the southwestern portion of New Zealand's South Island. A high mountain range runs north to south through the island, and cuts right through the center of Fiordland. These mountains are the result of two tectonic plates colliding. The Pacific Plate gets pushed up while the Australia Plate gets pushed under, creating the mountains in Fiordland known as the Southern Alps; and they are still rising about 2 centimeters (0.75 inches) per year. "As fast as your fingernails grow," as all the tour guides would tell us.

These mountains trap the hot, moist air blowing over the Tasman Sea from Australia, creating rainforests on the hills and snowfields on the peaks. During several ice ages of the past million years, massive glaciers formed over the Southern Alps, each gouging paths to the the sea as they expanded. The legacy of these now-melted glaciers is etched upon the dramatic, steep slopes of the fjords, some over a kilometer (about half a mile) from peak to water's edge, then dropping hundreds of meters further beneath the dark-blue surface.

We drove up through the winding alpine road, higher and higher, until forest disappeared and the snowline came closer. Just before the tunnel that ran through Homer Pass, we paused at a turn-off to soak in the dramatic view of the near-vertical granite mountains that soared on both sides of the road. It made me feel very small and very fragile. No wonder the roads closed during a storm. There would be no shelter here from an avalanche. I noticed the remains of a snowman at the roadside, built after a recent storm.

Through the dark, small tunnel, and out the other end, we emerged into Fiordland. The road now dropped steeply. Soon we were back in the rainforest. Rain — not snow — began to fall. To be honest, we have driven on far more treacherous roads in Austria and Norway, where I seriously feared for our lives, even when driving at 10 km per hour (6 mph). The Kiwis, however, build great, well-maintained roads through the wilderness. Of course, this particular road had to be built to handle the perpetual summertime traffic. In 2019 alone, 870,000 people visited Milford Sound, most of them traveling along this road via tour bus, car, or even camper van. Post-pandemic, the numbers are rising fast once more. It made me very happy we were arriving in mid-July — the dead of winter. We were the only car on the road for many miles.

Within half an hour of leaving the tunnel, we reached the water's edge of Milford Sound. Pulling into the parking lot, we faced the open fjord and there it was — that incredible iconic view of Mitre Peak, all the more beautiful for being shrouded in mist, right in front of us. The parking lot was nearly empty, the water placid and clear of traffic. At that point, so near to our arrival, we did not realize just how lucky we were to experience *quiet* in Milford Sound.

Misty Mitre Peak

We checked into the Milford Lodge, the only hotel in the fjord. The lodge is beautifully constructed of small brown-and-black box-shaped cabins that are almost invisible in the forest. We got a room overlooking the riverbank, with a view of the mountains outside our glass sliding doors. I went out for a hike in the light rain, just to get the lay of the land, and also to search for kea birds (see page C5).

At reception they told us please, please do not feed the kea, because feeding them turns them into beggars — not to mention that human food is bad for them. Kea are a rare, endangered species of alpine "land parrot." Unlike their more famous relative, the flightless kākāpo, kea can fly, but mostly they don't have to. They just walk around. Their feathers are a glimmering forest green to match their environment. Behavioral studies have shown them to be highly skilled at problem solving, with the intelligence level of a 4-year-old child. I don't know about other 4-year-olds, but my son Josh was one hell of a mischief-maker at 4. So are kea. A Milford kayak guide later told me kea sometimes show up by the launch area and wreak havoc on their gear. "They will destroy a running shoe in under ten minutes," he said.

At dusk, shortly after I returned from my walk, a pair of kea arrived right at our doorstep. They hung around our picnic table, looking for scraps. They found none, but discovered us, looking at them from the other side of the sliding door to our bedroom. They sauntered over to the glass for a closer look.

I wiggled my toes and one bird tapped at the glass with its beak, as if intent on nibbling the white sock on my foot. It stared right at my face, as if to say, "What's your deal, pal?" Its mate, however, read the room. It could tell we were not going to feed them and moved on towards the next cabin. The pair kind of reminded me of Teresa and me at a museum: I want to pore slowly over every exhibit; Teresa gets the general idea, then she's ready for the gift shop, no need to linger.

Tim bird: fascinated by a white sock. Teresa bird: "Nothing to see here; let's move it along."

I was enthralled by these feisty little birds, capable of surviving in this harsh alpine-fjord climate, and *choosing* to walk. Something in the back of my brain made me think I had heard of them before... *Monty Python*! The Dead Parrot sketch: "He's not dead... Perhaps he's pinin' for the fjords?" Oh My God — it wasn't a fictitious Norwegian Blue Parrot — the sketch could have been about a real kea parrot that actually does live in fjords!

The next morning we were booked for our cruise of Milford Sound on an early boat, to beat the daily tour-bus rush from Queenstown. It had rained hard that night, but now the sky was a bright cerulean blue. It was a bit of a shock to drive from our camouflaged cabin in the rainforest to the cruise-ship wharf. It looked like an airport terminal. It was the biggest building in Milford Sound, hosting close to a dozen tour booths, each with their own ship tied up outside on the wharf. In the summer season, each boat runs three two-hour cruises a day, and that's not counting larger ocean cruiseliners that pull into Milford Sound regularly throughout the summer. But we forgot all that the moment we stood on the wharf and looked out. We simply gaped at Mitre Peak, now fully visible (see page C17).

Our company, Cruise Milford, ran one of the smaller ships. The crowd was light that day. Perhaps the overnight closing of the road had discouraged others? With about 20 passengers aboard we motored the full length of the fjord to the Tasman Sea and back again. En route, we saw seals lolling on the rocks. Dolphins rose and dove next to us, splashing around playfully before taking off. Whales come into the fjord too, from time to time, our captain said, and even sharks.

Due to the recent rains, waterfalls streamed down the high cliffs on both sides of us, creating rainbows, and even a rain shower, when the captain deliberately maneuvered the ship right under one of the falls. Most of us fled the deluge, but a few hardy souls stayed out to photograph the inside of the falls, getting thoroughly drenched in the process.

Left: A cruise ship by a waterfall, dwarfed by the cliffs of Milford Sound (photo: Teresa Erickson). Right: I hope that smartphone is waterproof!

The next day I went kayaking with two other paddlers and one local guide, a big man with a bristly brown beard named Pauly. Mel and Andrew were Australians and had never kayaked before. Pauly told them this was not a problem. The weather was calm, and our sea kayaks were sturdy and stable. We floated along in no big rush to get anywhere fast, just enjoying being out on the calm, deep water.

At kayak-level, Milford Sound seemed a lot bigger and quieter than from the cruise-ship deck. The big boats had all departed up the fjord shortly after we hit the water, and soon we were in silence as we paddled. Then a plane flew in down the fjord and landed on the little airstrip that is hidden from the road. Pauly told us that during the summer, some 300 flights *per day* land and take off in Milford Sound; it's the fast and expensive way to get to the cruise ships from Queenstown.

"All day long, there's a roar of engines overhead," he told us. It was hard to imagine in this vast emptiness.

Pauly told us that the government had a master plan, Milford Opportunities, that calls for shutting down the airport and imposing a hefty charge on foreign tourists entering the fjord by the road. Later, I took a look at it online. The aim is to lessen the traffic (replacing cars with electric hop-on-hop-off buses) and increase the number of days visitors spend getting in and out of the fjord. Basically to slow the whole experience down.

Apparently the current tour operators are not happy with the government's grand plan, not at all! Pauly said there was a video about the controversy, called *Is Milford Sound Lost to Tourism?* which I also found online. Here are three of the most memorable quotes from the various officials and tour operators interviewed in the mini-documentary:

Tourism is an extractive industry. It uses the scenery and the extraordinary geography, but we don't get anything for it.

If you charge visitors, many of them will start going to other sounds — Doubtful and Dusky — that currently are pristine. Milford is already lost to tourism.

The solution isn't always to build a bigger car park.

Say a prayer for Milford Sound.

I could see both sides of the story. It was frankly surprising Milford Sound had so far not been destroyed by the tourist hordes. But I was not exposed to the congestion and exhaust fumes of the summer months. And who knows what damage the constant noise of air and sea traffic is causing both marine and land creatures? From my perch, as a visitor, I would have gladly paid a steep fee, knowing it was going to help preserve this wild land.

If you ever go to Milford Sound, please pause at the foot of Mitre Peak and just feel it: the sheer awe of standing in nature's grand cathedral. Then say a prayer for the master plan, and for the people with the passion and fortitude to preserve this place for the future.

Rangitoto: A tree anchoring an island of vegetation (Ch. 2)

A Northland beach in wintertime (Ch. 3)

Russell harbor, Bay of Islands (Ch. 3)

Hole in the Rock, Bay of Islands (Ch. 3)

Teresa among the kauri trees at Rainbow Falls (Ch. 4)

Waitangi Māori Cultural Center (top) and performers (bottom) (Ch. 5)

NZ birds: top left: kākāpo (critically endangered); top right: kiwi (endangered); lower left: kea (endangered; photo credit: Mel Mailler); lower right: tūi (ubiquitous; photo credit: Anne Bonfert)

Crystal-clear hot springs at Whakarewarewa, Rotorua (photo credit: Teresa Erickson) (Ch. 6)

Māori cultural performers demonstrating weapons training, Rotorua (Ch. 6)

The road to Mount Doom (Ngauruhoe) (Ch. 7)

Napier's Art Deco architecture (both pages) (Ch. 8)

The ridge forming the body of the giant Te Mata, looking east to the Pacific (Ch. 9)

Sunrise from our balcony at Kaiterikeri, the gateway to Abel Tasman Park (Ch. 11)

Left: Fern tree, Abel Tasman Park; top right: Māori water creature; middle right: Māori ancestor statue; bottom right: Māori decorated paddles on a beach walkway in the park (Ch. 11)

Pancake Rocks (Ch. 12)

Franz Josef Glacier seen from our helicopter (Ch. 13)

Teresa posing with our Polestar 2 on the shores of Lake Wakatipu (Ch. 14)

The view from Queenstown Peak (Ch. 14)

The steamship TSS *Earnslaw*, Queenstown (Ch. 14)

The many moods of Milford Sound (Ch. 15)

Mitre Peak (Ch. 15)

An old farmhouse sheltering from the winds in Catlins National Park (Ch. 19)

Curio Bay, Catlins National Park, with our beachhouse on the far left (Ch. 19)

Left: Tim at Steampunk HQ, Oamaru (Ch. 22). Right: Windswept road around the Otago Peninsula (Ch. 21)

The Bannockburn Sluicings: imagine it 160 years ago, with gold miners' tents pitched everywhere (Ch. 24)

Aoraki/Mount Cook, bigger than it looks (Ch. 25)

View of Lake Mueller from one of the bridges (Ch. 25)

Picture-perfect Lake Tekapo (Ch. 26)

Lake Tekapo from the observatories on Mount John (Ch. 26)

Christchurch Museum of Art (Ch. 27)

In Christchurch: A mural of a Māori woman holding a kingfisher and an owl (Ch. 27)

Māori ancestor statue guarding the entrance to Kaikōura (Ch. 29)

Kaikōura: As seen from my kayak: a sea lion flinging an octopus in the air, then swallowing it whole (Ch. 29)

Auckland: *Waharoa* by Māori artist Selwyn Frederick Muru (Ch. 32)

Pondering New Zealand's future (photo credit: Eric Bunge)

Chapter 16

Stargazing inside a Cave on Lake Te Anau

We sat in utter darkness in a little boat in the depths of a cave. Our guide had warned the 12 of us: no talking, don't make a sound, no photographs. It gave me an odd feeling of sensory deprivation. All I knew was that I was cold. I had lost track of Teresa's whereabouts on the boat, which was not much more than an aluminum shell with seats. Perhaps she was sitting next to me? I wasn't sure, and I was not about to grope around for her hand, lest I make a mistake and cause some poor Chinese tourist in our group to cry out in alarm. That would ruin the experience for everybody.

Our guide, sitting in the bow, slowly pulled the boat forward, deeper into the cave. He told us he would be drawing us through the darkness by pulling a wire cable secured to the cave wall. I could feel us surge forward a little. I stared up, into infinite nothingness, though I knew we were 200 meters (600 feet) deep inside a mountain, on a tiny lake within a large limestone cave.

To get this deep in the cave we first had to walk, slowly groping our way along a constructed metal walkway that followed the course of an underground river. Sometimes we had to hunch low where the cave roof shrank. Other times the walkway skirted the edge of gushing subterranean waterfalls, and once we passed through a wide cavern that had been lit to reveal high, yellow walls made of limestone, carved by water to resemble the interior of a miniature cathedral, with black water coursing down the main aisle.

"Are there any *fush* in the water?" I asked our guide (adroitly pronouncing "fish" with a New Zealand accent).

"No. Only eels. They grow pretty large here, as long as my leg."

Soon after that, the lights along the gangway ended, and we were compelled to climb down a steel ladder and then feel our way onto the boat in darkness and absolute silence.

Now that we were aboard and underway, our little boat seemed to turn a corner. Suddenly, I could see the stars above, though outside it was the middle of the afternoon. Bright pinpricks of bluish light seemed to move slowly overhead, though I knew full well it was us gliding past them on the roof of the cave, and not the other way around.

I was awed, and it was odd: experiencing this strange night sky, its unfamiliar constellations appearing so astronomically far away, even though I knew they were close — so close, in fact, that our guide recommended that however enraptured we became by these glowing stars, to keep our mouths shut, in case one of them should come unmoored from this false sky, and fall, as it easily might, into one of our gaping maws.

That would be gross. For these stars in the ersatz heavens were the famous New Zealand glow-worms. Worse, they are not even real worms: they are the larvae of a species of fungus gnat that breeds in caves and then lays its eggs on the roofs. Technically speaking, fly larvae are maggots, so these are actually *glow-maggots.*

When the larvae hatch, their bellies glow with intense bioluminescent light that attracts other insects that might have wandered into the cave — moths, mosquitoes, pretty much anything. To trap their prey, the glow-worms secrete "fishing lines": strands of sticky mucus that hang down several inches from the cave roof like miniature, gooey stalactites. With the touch of a wing, an insect gets glued to the mucus. The glow-worm sucks the fishing line back into itself, and then voraciously devours its prey. We were shown a video in the info center at the end of our little cave cruise that explained all this in graphic detail. Frankly, I was very glad to have seen these magnified images of the gnat maggots only *after* the mystical experience of the night-sky boat ride.

It was, however, quite fascinating. We learned these larvae live for about 90 days before metamorphosing into adult fungus gnats. The adult's single purpose is to have sex and reproduce. They have no mouth with which to eat. In fact, no digestive tract at all. If you are an adult gnat, you screw, lay eggs, and die. Afterward, a new generation of glow-worm larvae each stake out their square inch of territory on the roof, set out their fishing lines, and bedazzle the cave with their glowing bellies.

Ah, nature: weird, gross, and breathtakingly beautiful all at once.

The really amazing story, however, is how New Zealanders managed to turn staring at maggots in dank caves into a nationwide tourism craze. Teresa and I each paid about $50US for the glow-worm experience, which lasted for three hours, including the boat ride across Lake Te Anau to get to the cave.

Across New Zealand, there are dozens and dozens of commercial glow-worm tours, plus a great many more remote glow-worm caves one can visit on one's own. The biggest and most popular site, Waitomo, in the North Island, is a complex of some 400 glow-worm caves that gets approximately 500,000 visitors a year. Glow-worms have in fact metamorphosed into a multimillion-dollar tourism industry.

Of course, wherever there is industrial-scale tourism, there is also the risk of killing the gnat that lays the golden egg — or glowing maggot, to horrifically scramble the egg metaphor.

In the presence of light and noise, the startled glow-worms shut down their bioluminescence, ending the display, and preventing them from catching their prey. So the tour guides have to enforce strict protocols to ensure the glow-worms don't starve. There's no photography allowed at all (because too many idiot tourists don't know how to turn off the flash on their smartphones). Also, too much carbon dioxide, the wrong amount of humidity, or any introduced pollution can upset the delicate balance of the cave ecosystems the gnat larva requires to thrive. Tour operators have to monitor their operations and do whatever it takes to maintain the ecosystem's health.

In Waitomo, this has meant regulating the surrounding farmland, so that agricultural waste water does not contaminate the streams that feed the underground cave-lakes where the glow-worms live. As a result, certain areas are no longer used for crops or pasture and are conserved as wild spaces that keep the aquifer pure and the glow-worms glowing. Given the number of jobs created by the caves in this once-remote area, the farmers have complied. Good for the economy, good for the ecology. Good for the worms, good for the tourists.

This kind of positive cycle is called regenerative economics. Whereas modern capitalism seeks to extract the maximum dollar value from a system (with resulting negative externalities, such as pollution and land degradation), regenerative economics seeks to use resources in such a way as to create and maximize positive externalities (those that regenerate natural systems).

In researching this subject, I stumbled upon several great articles on regenerative economics from researchers working in New Zealand at the Edmund Hillary Fellowship. Backed by the Hillary Institute for International Leadership, the Fellowship funds pioneers and researchers dedicated to finding innovative scientific, cultural, social, and political solutions to today's problems. New Zealand is in many ways a perfect testing ground, in that it's a progressive democracy that knows it is facing big problems, including environmental ones. The nation also has the capacity to anticipate and respond, rather than react to events after the fact — or simply turn a blind eye, as all too many countries do.

To better deal with these urgent issues, the Fellowship recruits the best minds in the nation and the world — the intellectual equivalent of glow-worms, might we say? By generating new ideas that shine a light on the nation's problems, not only can new answers be discovered, but new innovative ecosystems — constellations of ideas — can be created. Solutions that show promise will be shared with other nations, which can adopt and adapt them to their own context.

Imagine, for a minute, visiting policymakers and heads of state in the metaphorical equivalent of aluminum boats, coming to New Zealand in order to gaze up at the Hillary Fellowship's human glow-worms, and their constellations of ideas for a future New Zealand, and a future world. You may gape in wonder as you contemplate the possibilities, with nary a fear that a luminescent maggot might drop into your open maw.

Chapter 17

Fiordland from a Floatplane

"I've never flown in a floatplane," Teresa confessed to me. This was to be her moment of opportunity! There is only one floatplane offering rides in all of New Zealand's South Island, and we had booked a one-hour flight on it during our stay in Te Anau, on our way back from Milford Sound. Frankly, I thought the cruise through the mountains of Milford Sound at sea level had been pretty amazing. Could anything more be gained from flying through Fiordland's mountains at eye level?

Ivan seemed to think so. He and his wife — pilots both — have built a successful local business ("Wings and Water") providing this unique view from their little four-seater. Climbing aboard, one couldn't help but notice that a floatplane is basically built out of aluminum foil. A thin layer of the light-but-strong metal reduces the weight of the plane while keeping it just sturdy enough that the wings don't fall off. It seems rather like flying in a paper airplane with a propeller.

'I thought it would be... bigger," my beloved said, her voice quivering only a tad as she took her seat next to me. It had been weeks since we had taken a helicopter trip over Franz Josef Glacier, and Teresa had spent much of that flight with her eyes squeezed shut. One of the things I love about Teresa is that she never lets fear stand in the way of a new adventure. Hence, here she is, once again strapping herself in next to me in a flimsy flying contraption. Fortunately, Ivan inspires confidence. He told us he has two young daughters, and with his wife away flying in Australia this summer, the parenting is all on him. I doubted he would take off if he wasn't 100% confident he would be home to cook his girls' dinner.

Ivan takes off from Lake Te Anau.

Up we soared, into the sky and over the town of Te Anau (population 1857). On the ground, this town at the edge of the magnificent Fiordland wilderness seemed frightfully dull. It reminded me of a US suburb from the 1950s: a lot of one-story bungalows with big, flat lawns. But from the air, in full view of the surrounding peaks, it looked dazzling!

Left: The view towards Milford Sound, looking across Lake Te Anau. Right: U-shaped glacier valley

We flew across Lake Te Anau, the largest lake in the whole South Island. Looking down over the opposite shore we got a glimpse of the Hidden Lakes — deep, black pools left behind by the glaciers that covered the South Island, not just once but five times in the past million years.

Turning up one finger of the lake, we headed towards the Fiordland mountains. From this vantage, it was so easy to see how the glaciers had carved out the valleys into their classic U shape. As the mountains climbed, so did we, staying at about snow level. From here we could see the treeline, and follow the path of waterfalls from streams emerging from the ice to where they plunged into the still waters below. Ivan pointed out bald strips in the high forests. These were tree avalanches, he told us. These big trees grow right in the rock — there's no soil, just a carpet of moss and debris for the roots to cling to. Every now and then, one tree falls, dragging many others down with it, tearing a scar across the slope that takes decades to heal.

We threaded our way between the mountaintops. It was mesmerizing, like my dreams of flying, where I'm hanging in space, suspended by nothing yet gliding forward. I could have stayed like this for the rest of my life, and at that moment I envied Ivan (despite his childcare responsibilities). I looked over at Teresa. Eyes open, she gazed out the window, lost to the beauty of the mountains. That made me smile. Eventually, we popped out of the high hills and onto Lake Manapouri, the second-largest lake in Fiordland, also surrounded by wilderness, except where it touched the road and the village which shares its name.

Ivan had promised us a landing here, and a walk on a remote beach. We banked and curved into a falling arc across the sky. (At this point, I noticed Teresa closed her eyes, but only for a brief minute.) The plane leveled and Ivan skimmed down over the glassy surface of the lake so smoothly we could not tell the exact moment the floats touched the water. Ivan helped us off the plane and onto the beach. This, he told us, was his favorite, hidden spot.

On the beach, I found tracks in the sand that looked like large backward arrows. They seemed fresh.

"This is a kiwi!" Ivan exclaimed, astonished. "I've been coming here for seven years, and never seen kiwi tracks on any of these beaches!"

We knew what a good sign this was, as introduced weasels, ferrets, and stoats have decimated kiwi and other flightless birds across New Zealand. Why would anyone in their right mind bring predators to these islands? They were intentionally imported to reduce the exploding rabbit population. Rabbits were brought here by the early settlers for food and hunting for sport. Released into the wild, with no natural predators, rabbits multiplied so rapidly that they began degrading the pasturelands that had been cleared for sheep. Thus ferrets, stoats, and weasels were shipped to New Zealand as an early attempt at biological control — one that went very, very badly.

The introduced predators found the native birds and their eggs much easier prey than the rabbits. The kiwi and their flightless friends had no instinctive defenses or wariness of land predators. They were sitting ducks. Thus began 150 years of extirpation. Some birds went extinct. Others, like the famous flightless parrot, the kākāpo, have survived only by being transplanted to a few islands that have been cleared of all predators. The kākāpo are gradually rebuilding their numbers into the hundreds under the intensive care watch of teams of devoted conservationists (see page C5).

The very good news is that some of these endangered birds are making a comeback, literally from the brink of extinction. The kiwi, too. While their numbers are still declining by about 2% per year across the country, in areas with extensive predator control and active measures to assist the incubation of eggs and rearing of chicks, the numbers are increasing.

In fact, the government has announced an aspirational goal of a predator-free New Zealand by 2050, which will allow the native birds to flourish everywhere. I've not run into anyone who thinks that goal is realistic. But it shows a radical shift in mindset and priorities in modern New Zealand. In fact, I don't think I've come across another nation so committed to conservation. Sure, after 150 years of environmental destruction, the descendants of European settlers have much to atone for. But they are atoning. That, at least, is the message of hope I read in those kiwi tracks on this remote Fiordland beach.

Kiwi tracks on a beach near Te Anau

Chapter 18

Why We Travel with Endangered Birds in Our Car

There is a perfectly rational explanation as to why we travel with endangered birds in our car. It all started with the kiwi.

Teresa and I became enamored with kiwis from the get-go of our New Zealand trip. When we arrived in Russell, the lush, tiny town in the remote north of the North Island, we discovered kiwis lived in the brush surrounding our cottage. Every night we could hear them calling. You could say they had us at "Keweeeeeeeeeee! Keweeeeeeeeeee! Keweeeeeeeeeee!"

The call of the female kiwi is very like the battle cry you might unleash if you were a Viking shield maiden in combat, hacking at dire enemies with an ax. The shriek gets louder and rises in pitch at the end of each call. At first, it was downright freaky to hear this sound right off our deck. Once we realized what it was, and could imagine these adorable, hairy-feathered birds stalking in our grounds at night, we began to enjoy the terrifying sound, though we pitied the hapless males! If that's the call female kiwis make when they're feeling amorous, what must they sound like when they're angry?

Teresa claimed she spotted a kiwi on the road our very first evening in Russell. I was skeptical. Kiwis are relatively rare compared to the other flightless birds in Russell. Pūkeko (swamp hens) and weka (wood hens) abound in the area, and they are both about the same size as kiwis — as big as a chicken. I found those other birds were everywhere when I went for a walk at dusk.

But Teresa was adamant: "It walked like a kiwi."

"Oh, so you know how a kiwi walks?"

"They have a very distinctive walk. They scooch their butts."

"Is that the *ornithological* term for it?"

Teresa tilted her head to the side, those big brown eyes flashing, and spoke to me in a tone of mild surprise.

"Tim, you mistakenly seem to think I give a rat's ass about whether or not you believe me. I know what I saw, and I saw a kiwi. It scooched its butt."

Did I mention that Teresa is the most self-referenced person I know? It's part of her charm, I tell myself.

Two weeks later, in Rotorua, I visited a kiwi conservation and recovery center that features a darkened enclosure where one can view kiwis behind glass. They also run a hatching and rearing operation that cares for kiwi chicks and returns them to the wild when they are big enough to fight off predators (stoats, rats, cats, and possums only eat the eggs and chicks). A grown kiwi might look adorable, but its clawed feet and strong legs make it a fierce fighter. Kiwi egg-recovery programs take eggs from the wild, raise the chicks, then release them when they are big enough to fend for themselves. This boosts their odds of survival from less than 5% to 65%.

Fun Kiwi Facts:

- Kiwis lay the largest egg of all birds — proportional to their body size: about six times as big as a chicken egg, and one-third as big as a female kiwi. Ouch! Once she lays her massive egg, the mama kiwi's job is done. The male kiwi does all the incubating.
- The kiwi's egg contains almost twice as much yolk as other eggs, nourishing the growing chicks so well that they hatch fully feathered and independent.
- Soon after hatching, the young kiwi leaves the nest. There's virtually no parenting or protection, since the kiwi evolved in a land with no natural predators.

- Kiwi feathers are long and hairlike, and they exude a pungent oil that covers the feathers to keep them clean as they hunt insects on the forest floor. Unfortunately, that strong smell makes them easy to find for introduced mammalian predators like stoats, cats, and dogs.

Teresa declined to join me on the kiwi tour ("I don't need to see *another* kiwi"), which is too bad, because she probably would have enjoyed the look on my face as I watched a little kiwi run about the dimly lit enclosure. It scooched its butt. There are no other words to express it.

Left: A kiwi road sign. Right: Kiwi from the Otago Museum in Dunedin, perhaps preserved mid-scooch?

As the newly established kiwi expert on our team, Teresa found a way to bring her knowledge to bear as we drove across the North Island. She doesn't like to drive on the wrong side of the road, and so she co-pilots. Part of her job is to keep me awake if I get drowsy behind the wheel. Her imitation of a female kiwi proved a highly effective technique. It jolted me upright better than a Red Bull. She would also shriek like a kiwi if we passed a road sign warning of danger ahead.

This was hilarious at first, but it really did spike my cortisol levels. I pleaded with her to please go back to poking me in the ribs to keep me alert at the wheel. Not long after that, at a gift shop in Wellington, we found a bin full of little stuffed kiwis that shrieked if you squeezed them. It was a very chirpy, kid-friendly version of a kiwi shriek. And so we bought one and put it to work in our car. On passing a danger sign, Teresa would simply squeeze the kiwi and its happy squeak would keep me focused.

Okay, so that explains the kiwi — but what about the *parrot*?

We grew quite fond of our kiwi, so fond that we felt neglectful when we left it in the car overnight. Then, at Milford Sound, as you may recall, we encountered our first kea.

Kea playing with Tim's toe… or trying to bite it off? (See also page C5)

Fun Kea Facts:

- Experiments on kea show they are capable of solving the kinds of complex problems only great apes (like us) can manage, for example, applying principles of probability.

- Though kea can fly, they spend most of their time walking (perhaps that's why I like them?). They also nest on the ground, which makes them easy prey for stoats and feral cats.
- There's no accurate count of how many kea are left, because they live in wild, remote habitats — dense beech forests and steep mountain slopes — where it is difficult for researchers to get to. The estimated number is 3000–7000.
- There used to be a bounty on them. Kea were the scourge of sheep farmers because they would sit on top of sheep and peck at the fat in their backs. Ugh. The sheep would get infections and die.

You will recall that two kea sauntered across our cottage deck in Milford Sound, coming right up to the sliding glass door. I have no doubt they would have strolled right on in if the door was open, for they have no fear of humans. Imagine a pair of feral 4-year-olds with wire cutters for teeth peering in at you! One looked right at me and then kept tapping its beak at my foot on the other side of the glass. Did it think my white sock was food, or was it playing a game with me? I just loved that brave and feisty little bird.

"Timothy — do *not* open that sliding door!" Teresa said severely.

She seldom uses my full name, invoking childhood memories of my mother when she was deadly serious and there was to be no clowning around. It's very effective. I suggested we take the kea with us in the car to keep our kiwi company, but Teresa would not play that little game with me. The kea on the other side of the glass door soon got bored and wandered off to join its mate.

However, the next day, at a Department of Conservation gift shop, we encountered a bin filled with all the stuffed wild birds of New Zealand, each with its own call when you squeezed it, including, of course, a kea.

So now, our kiwi has a friend, and they travel together with us in the console of our spiffy Polestar 2, between the front seats. We squeeze them hello in the morning, and whenever something exciting happens — plus of course, the kiwi still shrieks to keep me alert when there's danger on the road ahead.

Why we travel with endangered birds

It is all we can do not to buy more of them… a little blue penguin? A tūi? A kākāpo? But we know, that way madness lies. If we buy one more, we will have opened the floodgates to the whole menagerie. How would we explain at customs that we are traveling with a suitcase full of endangered New Zealand birds?

Chapter 19

Penguin Spotting in the Catlins

The Catlins in wintertime seemed to be the land tourism forgot. The main tourist track through the South Island hits Queenstown, Milford Sound, and Aoraki/Mount Cook. Catlins Forest Park, however, is about 200 kilometers (125 miles) further south. In fact, the Catlins coast is as far south as you can get on the South Island. We only learned about the place thanks to a friendly Californian woman we met at a café near Auckland. She had lived in New Zealand for two decades. On recognizing our North American accents, she decided to offer some travel advice. She borrowed a pen and a napkin and wrote out for us half a dozen must-see spots for us, including the Catlins. We carried that napkin with us for over 1500 kilometers (900 miles).

From Te Anau, on the edge of Fiordland, we drove south and east through the flat farming region called Southlands, through endless beige pastures filled with innumerable beige sheep. Gradually the land got hillier, the farms smaller, the road rougher. Eventually, we hit a signpost announcing we had entered the Catlins Scenic Coastal Highway. Scenic, yes. Highway? Not so much. It was paved; that's about all I can say for it. We found very little in the way of visitor infrastructure. Brown signposts indicated spots of interest for tourists: remote lighthouses, beaches, and viewpoints along the route. Other than that, nothing. And yet this was one of the most alluring, charming, and wild parts of New Zealand (see page C18).

On the last stretch to our Air B&B for the night in Curio Bay, the highway passed between a wetland and a lagoon. Suddenly, the road itself went *underwater*. The tide was coming in, and the water covered the road for about the length of a tennis court. A small sign informed us that the road might be impassable at times. Well, *that* would have been a nice warning to have had way back where the "Scenic Highway" began.

Teresa at the Nugget Point Lighthouse, Catlins

Checking the map, I was dismayed to see that backtracking and going around on an inland road would be a 100-kilometer

(60-mile) detour. I didn't have it in me. I took a long look at the incoming tide. If the submerged part of the road was flat, it couldn't be more than 6 inches (15 cm) deep. But the longer we dithered, the deeper the water.

"What's the worst that could happen?" I pondered aloud.

Teresa had a ready answer: "You don't actually *know* how deep the water is! It could fry the battery in our EV. And — we haven't seen another car on the road for miles."

I hit the accelerator.

"*This* is how we *die!*" said Teresa, covering her eyes.

Ocean water sprayed to the left and the right in a rather alarming wake as I held a straight course for dry land ahead. What if there was a little zigzag in the road? Well, I hadn't thought of that. And, most fortunately, neither had the road builders. In under a minute, we made it back to gravel on the other side. Teresa was strangely silent. Certain death averted, *for now.*

Ten minutes further down the road, we reached our destination. Our little beachhouse at Curio Bay was one of about 30 cottages stretched out behind the dunes along a long crescent beach. In the dead of winter — early August — the beach was deserted. While much of the vegetation remained green in winter, grassy tussocks had turned rust red in the dunes, contrasting sharply with the white sand, the navy blue of the sea, and the indigo twilight sky.

Our hosts told us that little blue penguins — *kororā*, as the Māori call them — nested in the dunes. Some even made their homes right under our deck! If we watched out for them at dusk or dawn, supposedly we could see them make the walk to and from the ocean each day. These are the tiniest penguins in the world, about 1 kilogram on average (about 2.5 pounds), and only 30 centimeters (1 foot) tall.

Despite our twilight vigil, we never saw so much as a flipper. However, we did hear them. When the little blue penguins settle in for the night, they like to chatter with their neighbors. They are very sociable birds. Their chitchat, however, is conveyed by screeching. It sounded as if cats were being murdered in the dunes.

Next morning, we drove to the end of the Curio Bay Road, which has two exciting features in one locale: a petrified forest on the shore, and a "penguin walk" for another species of penguin that makes its home in the Catlins: the *hoiho* — or yellow-eyed penguin. These are some of the rarest, most endangered penguins in the world, with a remaining population of just 6000–7000 birds, mostly found on sub-Antarctic islands owned by New Zealand.

The mainland population is down to about 220 breeding pairs. Worse, that number has been in decline for three decades due to disease, entanglement in fishing nets, loss of coastal forest habitat, and introduced predators — including dogs — when tourists let them off the leash near penguin nesting grounds. Curio Bay is one of the few remaining hoiho havens on the mainland. The lone operator of the surprisingly new information-center-cum-café told us it was not breeding season, so there were no young in the nests, and that meant even fewer adults might come ashore here this time of year.

The coastline at the bluff of Curio Bay is itself a geological marvel: it's a petrified Jurassic forest. The info center explains that about 180 million years ago a volcano erupted nearby, covering an old forest with ash. Massive floods after the eruption washed over the ruined forest, burying it in sediment. The ash and sediment infused the dead wood with silica and petrified it. Over the subsequent millennia, waves scoured away the sediment, exposing the hard rock of the petrified forest along 20 kilometers (12 miles) of coastline. At first, I couldn't see it. It just looked like jumbled dark-brown stone, like any other rocky shore. But after a while my eyes adjusted. Suddenly I could see those jutting rocks were stumps; those elongated slabs were fallen trunks. What one moment looked normal to me seemed suddenly otherworldly: the deep past, frozen in time.

Left: Model kororā, or little blue penguin. Right: Model hoiho, or yellow-eyed penguin. (My photos from the Otago Museum)

Jurassic Beach: Curio Bay's petrified forest

I returned that evening to see if I could spy a few hoiho coming ashore. It was freezing cold and windy. A young Irish couple, Cormac and Chantelle, kept the frigid vigil with me. Like Teresa and me, they were traveling around the country. But not like us, they were staying in a camper van. Ah, youth! As dusk settled, a single hoiho emerged from the ocean about 100 meters (300 feet) away from us. Slowly it waddled its way through the petrified forest and up to the shore. We saw it turn, pause, and cast its yellow eyes back to the water, as if waiting for something. More penguins, perhaps? I was gripped by the sad thought that one day, the last yellow-eyed penguin in the world would pull itself from the waves, look back… and never see another of its kind again.

***

I had a second chance to see the little blue penguins a week later. An enterprising eco-venture outfit had built a kororā-viewing platform near a small beach on Taiaroa Head, at the end of the Otago Peninsula where we were then staying. Though not endangered, the kororā are in decline, with a total population of around 350,000–600,000 birds. The biggest threats to kororā are dogs, yes, but even worse, cars! The penguins travel up to 200 meters (600 feet) inland, often crossing roads at dusk. They are small, fast, and hard to see. New Zealand is the only place in the world where I've seen "Penguins Crossing" road signs.

In summer, during nesting season, some 300 kororā shelter here. But now, in midwinter, we were told to expect around 20–30 birds. That's enough for an exciting hour's viewing on a freezing-cold evening. In fact that evening was the coldest I experienced in New Zealand. Heck, I don't remember the last time I was so cold. And I'm a *Canadian*. The powerful offshore wind seemed to come up from Antarctica and blow right through me. My several layers of warm clothing might as well have been lace curtains on an open window. I huddled behind the wooden boards of the penguin-viewing barricade with about 30 other shivering viewers, and waited for the penguins to come ashore.

The little penguins began popping up out of the water in small teams of three to eight birds. Each cluster would race up the bank, right below us, and then disappear into the tufts of tussocks where they had their nests (safety in numbers, apparently). The penguin-program facilitators told us the penguins don't fear us humans behind the wooden barricades of the viewing station, because they see us as safely caged. Indeed, they seemed totally oblivious to our presence.

We watched them clamber ashore. To run, they have to flap their tiny flippers in opposite directions, so their whole body careens from side to side as they race forward. Every now and then, one would stop and stretch out its tiny wings in the freezing wind and shake the water off its sleek white belly and shiny blue back — yes, they are actually navy blue! I could sense how comfortable, happy even, they were in that intense cold wind, wind that was turning me into a popsicle. I felt such admiration for these little birds: so tiny, so tough, so fearless.

I realized how very much I want to live in a world with plenty of penguins. Don't you?

Chapter 20

A Scottish Castle on the Otago Peninsula

From time to time as we traveled New Zealand, Teresa would gaze at a craggy, gray mountain, or a blue, loch-shaped lake, or a green hillside filled with sheep, and exclaim "This looks *exactly* like Scotland!" We both love that far-off, wild country that is so similar in so many ways to this land down under that many Scots actually emigrated here more than 150 years ago. Numerous New Zealand place names reveal the attachment of Scottish New Zealanders to their land of origin, such as Eskdale, Cape Campbell, Ardmore, and Glenorchy — to name just a few out of more than a hundred.

But on a high hill in the remote and windswept Otago Peninsula, near the oh-so-Scottish city of Dunedin, one can find the most Scottish place in all of New Zealand: a stone castle, complete with ghost, supposedly, and a tragic tale of the wealthy family who once lived there. Larnach Castle is, in fact, the only castle in all of New Zealand. Indeed, why would anyone construct a castle here? This was not a medieval fortress, built to withstand English sieges and cannon fire. It was a family mansion — a folly, if you will — built by William Larnach, of Scottish ancestry, who became one of New Zealand's richest and most powerful men until his death in the late 1800s.

The road to the mountaintop on which the castle stands is perhaps one of the narrowest and windiest we have driven in all of New Zealand. The Otago Peninsula is riddled with volcanic hills from ancient eruptions, and so the landscape seems designed more for sheep than cars. Eventually, we reached the flat top of the mountain, where steep-sloped pastures gave way to forest. We passed through an entrance gate, parked, then walked through a dark wood for several minutes in order to reach the majestic, manicured lawn at the perimeter of the castle grounds.

We laughed aloud when we first saw it. This building was simply incongruous here on the edge of the South Pacific. From the massive stone lions at the front steps, up the severe granite walls to the crenelated turrets, the whole edifice seemed conjured right out of *Macbeth*.

Larnach Castle

We climbed the stone stairway and paid our admission for the self-guided tour through the 25 rooms of the castle. The entire basement floor was dedicated to the Larnach family history: a drama indeed worthy of Shakespeare. We wondered why some New Zealand TV station had not yet made a miniseries about their lives?

As a young man, William Larnach worked as a banker in Australia's gold fields: his first "bank" consisted of a tent and several strongboxes, made secure by his dogs and a gun. Helped by his family connections, he moved to New Zealand to take on the position of branch manager at the Bank of Otago in Dunedin before he was 30. Leveraging his ability to borrow from his own bank, Larnach became a land speculator. He bought sheep farms, timber mills, and hardware operations, amassing both riches and debts along the way.

With his newfound wealth, Larnach commissioned the castle as a private residence for his wife Eliza and their growing family. Materials from all over the world were brought to the mountaintop: marble from Italy, slate from Wales, ceramic tiles from England, glass from Venice and France. New Zealand native woods were used throughout the interior: kauri tree ceilings, rimu floors, and honeysuckle paneling. It took 200 men three years to build the structure, and a dozen more years for a team of expert European craftsmen to finish the interior.

Larnach went on to become a politician and cabinet minister. Though living in unimaginable splendor by New Zealand standards, in true Scottish fashion, tragedy dogged the wealthy Larnach clan. Eliza died young, at age 38, leaving six children behind. Larnach soon remarried — to Eliza's younger sister, Mary, which seems most odd. Supposedly, his reasoning was that Aunt Mary knew all the children well, and so could slip quite comfortably into the role of their mother. Apparently, the kids hated her.

Five years later, Mary died in turn. A few years after that, at the age of only 20, Larnach's favorite daughter, Kate, succumbed to cancer. Larnach had just finished adding a ballroom to his castle just for Kate — a ballroom in which she never had a chance to dance. A third time Larnach married, this time to a much younger woman, Constance de Bathe Brandon. She — so the story goes — ended up having an affair with one of Larnach's now-adult sons. Plagued by depression, William Larnach shot himself and died in his parliamentary offices in 1898.

Larnach left most of his estate to Constance. But the will was contested by his children, who ultimately won in court. They sent the dispossessed third wife packing. Constance left the castle and never returned, living out her days in Wellington. She never remarried, and did not end up with William's adulterous son, even though he alone took her side when the will was contested.

None of the family lived in the castle after that, but neither could they sell it. No one wanted to buy it. Who could afford it? Eventually, it was taken over by the state. All the fine furniture and furnishings were sold at auction and the place was stripped bare. In the first decades of the twentieth century, it was used variously as a "lunatic" asylum, a hospital for shell-shocked soldiers, and a nunnery. For a time, Kate's ballroom was turned into a sheep-holding pen.

The moldering castle passed from owner to owner, and at times sat abandoned. Only in the 1960s did the Barker family have the crazy vision to buy it, restore it, refurbish it, and turn it into a hotel and tourist attraction. They transformed the stables and workers' quarters into guest rooms. In the evenings, visitors can dine in grand style on the gleaming wood table in the castle dining room. The Barkers have been running the place for 60 years now.

I think the new owners don't seem to mind the reputation the castle has as one of the most haunted places in New Zealand because it attracts tourists. The haunting is driven home rather pointedly during the house tour. As Teresa and I entered Constance's bedroom on the second floor, our eyes were immediately drawn to the ceiling, where a woman with dark hair and bluish skin hovered in the air, wearing nothing but her Victorian-era undergarments.

Clearly, she was meant to be a ghost. But whose? Both Mary and Eliza also had this room as their personal space. None of the furnishings that fill the room are original to the castle; remember, it was stripped bare when the Larnachs left. It's been redone with period furnishings, paintings, exhibits of what a lady's room would have looked like — and also a few other, rather creepy mannequins to match the one floating in the air. One is a gray-haired, dour woman. She sits on a chair, embroidering a placemat. Another mannequin is a pretty young woman wearing a white wedding dress. It's believed this was the dress young Constance actually wore on the happy day of her nuptials. She's encased in glass, frozen like a museum specimen. Her skin is eerily ashen; her free hand looks black and dead as it hovers above her faded wedding bouquet. I knew she was only made of plaster, but her face seemed so lifelike in its stillness, her flat eyes capturing a look both haughty and resigned.

One dark and stormy night, Teresa and I returned to the castle for dinner. It was my sixty-fifth birthday, and I wanted to celebrate in style. Three other couples showed up for supper in the great hall, and while the rain poured down on the castle walls, we all ate and drank heartily, toasting the birthday boy.

After dinner, Shannon, the duty manager that evening, asked us if we had any questions about the castle. I took my opportunity to inquire about the supposed ghosts. She verified that yes, there were stories of a man in whiskers being glimpsed — doubtless William Larnach. There were strange knockings in the middle of the night. One guest claimed to have been pushed by an invisible force, not once, but three times.

"But what about the ghost on the ceiling of Constance's room?" I persisted. "Is that supposed to be... *her*?"

"It's hard to say," she replied uneasily.

"But what do *you* think?"

"Well, if there is a ghost in that room, then it's certainly *Mary*," she blurted out. "In fact, it's the only room in the castle I won't enter!" She paused, suddenly flushed.

Unbidden, into the silence, another guest spoke.

"I saw my dead husband once."

Heather was here at the castle with her *second* husband. We all swiveled our necks to look at her.

"I opened the bedroom door and he was just standing there, real as life. This was not long after he died. I never saw him again…" Her voice trailed off into a long and awkward silence.

Personally, I've never experienced anything that could best be explained by ghosts. But two people who are very credible, very close to me, have: my sister and Teresa. I take their experiences seriously, and so I don't dismiss the idea lightly. I asked Teresa on the ride back whether or not she felt the castle was haunted.

"'Haunted' would be the wrong word," she told me. "Not 'ghosts' as people typically think about them. But there is a presence in the castle. I felt that. Something lingers."

Left: A ghost hovers in Constance's room. Right: After dinner at Larnach Castle: it looks as if we are all set for a game of Clue! (Tim and Teresa, center)

Chapter 21

Encounters with Albatrosses at Taiaroa Head

Whenever the subject of albatrosses comes up in conversation, Teresa and I look at each other and shriek "Albatross!" We do it in the distinctive British accent of John Cleese. The absurd *Monty Python* sketch in which Cleese attempts to sell a dead albatross at a theater as an intermission snack is seared into our memories. My one other point of reference for the great bird is, of course, Coleridge's epic poem, *The Rime of the Ancient Mariner*, in which the mariner maliciously kills an albatross and is forced to wear its carcass around his neck until he atones for his crime.

Thus, none of my encounters with albatrosses have ever been with live ones. That changed when I arrived at the Otago Peninsula.

"Albatross!"

Once, this whole area was a volcano that erupted and left behind a great circular cone of igneous rock. Over millions of

years, wind and wave and rain wore crevasses into the rock, until it eroded into a land of fractured cliffs, dramatic bluffs, and strange, geometrical formations. The bluff at the very end of the peninsula is called Taiaroa Head. At the top of the cliffs is a grassy slope, buffeted by perpetual ocean winds. This is the world's only mainland nesting ground for albatrosses; most of these magnificent birds nest on remote island atolls, far away from humans and other predators.

Taiaroa Head

Albatrosses are some of the largest oceangoing seabirds in the world. In fact, one species, the wandering albatross, has the world's largest recorded wingspan at 12.1 feet (3.7 meters) — wider than a condor. They use those big wings to glide on strong ocean winds. The species at Taiaroa Head, the northern royal albatross, made the unusual choice to nest on the bluff over a century ago, when it was a military outpost during the First World War. Of course, soldiers and animals alike ate the eggs — they were easy pickings. Yet, the albatrosses persisted until 1936, when a young biology professor, Lance Richdale, who was studying local penguin populations, stumbled upon an albatross at Taiaroa Head sitting on an egg. He returned a few days later, and found the egg gone. He knew someone or something had stolen or eaten that egg. For Lance, it was a life-changing moment. He vowed to make sure the next albatross to nest at Taiaroa Head would see its chick live!

Lance became the driving force in setting up predator traps. He got the army to install fences around the bluff to keep people and dogs away. Lance even camped in a tent beside the next albatrosses that nested on the bluff (they have no fear of humans). He guarded and studied the birds, recording their rearing habits. Of the four nests he found in 1937, only one egg was hatched, but due to Lance's dogged determination, that chick survived and fledged. Lance's first scientific publication on the species was soon fledged too, launching his lifelong career studying and protecting the Taiaroa Head albatrosses.

Eighty-five years later, some 30 pairs of albatross nest each year on Taiaroa Head, and the research station built by Lance has passed the 500 mark for the number of birds fledged. Given that the northern royal albatross is an endangered species with fewer than 17,000 adults in the world, this is a huge deal.

Albatrosses Research Center monitors, protects, and nurtures the young birds. They also run a fantastic "albatross experience" tour for visitors, taking them up to a glassed-in viewing station right in the midst of the nests. The blustery August afternoon that I took the tour, there were four large chicks visible about 20–40 meters (60–120 feet) away. Each young albatross — a ball of white fluff about the size of large turkey — waited patiently for its parents to return with fish to feed them.

According to our guide, an enthusiastic young researcher named Francesca, when fully grown, these chicks' wingspans will surpass 3 meters (9 feet), and they will fly an astounding 190,000 kilometers (120,000 miles) each year of their adult lives. She pointed out the occasional adult as it soared by the viewing station. We also saw seagulls and shags struggling to fly straight in the buffeting winds, their wings all flappy-flappy. Not the albatrosses. They soared, smooth and steady, through gusts that probably would have knocked me off my feet if I were not behind a glass wall. It was thrilling to watch them. Francesca told us to focus on their webbed feet. We could see them twitch and wobble, which is how the birds steer as they glide.

One of the coolest things about observing the chicks in August is that they are getting close to fledging, which means they spend a lot of time on the ground stretching and flapping their wings to strengthen them for their first flight. Francesca explained that at this stage, the young birds weigh about 10 kilograms (22 pounds), and require a lot of food to keep growing. So both parents leave their chicks unattended while they search for fish.

It's hard enough for a big albatross to fly all day and feed itself. But to feed another bird nearly as big as you, one that just sits around all day in the nest playing video games and texting its friends when it should be stretching and preparing for life on the wing... well, parenting a teenage albatross takes everything out of you. Literally. The young bird nuzzles the adults' throats in a way that makes them regurgitate food. Vomited fish! Yum. Feeding goes on like this for eight whole months before the day comes when the young bird stretches its wings fully, and for the first time lifts off and soars into the sky.

Francesca said the newly fledged birds do not return after first flight. They fly straight off to Patagonia — a 10,000-km (6000-mile) journey — to feast on octopus and squid. They eventually fly back to Taiaroa several years later to find a mate, lay an egg, and become parents themselves.

"So, they never even say goodbye to their parents?" I asked. "When they return to Taiaroa Head, do you ever see them, um, *visit* their parents?"

Francesca seemed confused by the question.

"No, once they fledge, there's no bond. They just fly off and live their lives."

Personally, I'd be pissed off if I vomited into my child's mouth for all those months and he never so much as dropped by to say "Thanks for all the fish." But perhaps I am over-identifying with albatross parents?

These young birds are pretty lucky that, as well as their parents, they have a team of researchers looking after them. Sometimes, if one of the parents doesn't return from the sea — dies, that is — the researchers will step in and handfeed it to supplement what the single parent provides. (No vomiting, though.) If both parents fail to return, leaving an egg behind, the researchers have even had success fostering it with another pair of albatrosses whose egg has cracked or is infertile. Meanwhile, the predator control program is a success, so much so that the local little blue penguin colony on the beach below is flourishing too.

The albatross remains endangered, nonetheless. The hazards they face are mostly human caused. They get tangled in fishing nets, hooked by the long-line fishing lines that float on the oceans, and worst of all, they eat bits of plastic waste that accumulate in massive quantities in the oceans, even in the remote South Pacific. The Albatross Research Center features a grisly display of the several pounds of plastic found in a dead albatross's stomach: everything from little plastic toys and bottle caps to a toothbrush. The plastic fills up their guts. They can't excrete it, so, bellies bloated, they starve to death.

It's easy to be cynical about human nature. We've done horrible things to the living creatures on the planet we share, and driven many species to the brink of extinction. Like the Ancient Mariner, we all have dead albatrosses slung around our necks. But here on Taiaroa Head, a community of people, inspired by Lance, are helping to ensure a secure future for this great bird. If there's hope for the albatross, there might yet be hope for us, too.

Albatross aloft, and four white chicks visible dots on the bluff below

Chapter 22

Steampunk Time Warp to Oamaru

As we stepped through the portal, the walls, floor, and ceiling dropped away, leaving us suspended in infinity on the metal gangway. Streamers of multicolored lights fell away in all directions. We were no longer in New Zealand, but rather in some alternate dimension.

Or so it seemed. My partner, the fearless Tess Torridon (who sometimes goes by the alias "Teresa"), plucked at my sleeve. She guided us back towards the portal's iron door. An instant later, we found ourselves in a cavernous stone warehouse full of strange machines and menacing robot animals: a scrap-metal gorilla, a giant rust-red crab, an extinct moa bird, with gears in its eyes and hips.

Left: Transported to another dimension. Right: Rampaging mechanical gorilla from the menagerie

Intrepid Tess found a passageway out of the mechanical menagerie through a steel door labeled HB/1. We stumbled through the darkness, finally emerging into the intense bright sunlight of a New Zealand winter. For a minute we thought we had returned to the normal world. But no, we were in a courtyard surrounded by even more fantastic machines: an alien-catching crane, a dirigible suspended in the air above our heads, and a cannon with a door on the side (clearly designed for human transport). Dominating the courtyard was a rusted train car kitted out with drills and spears that ran on spiked wheels like something out of *Mad Max*. Iron figures in the shapes of tormented humans appeared among the rusted machines. Were they taunting us, or warning us that this was a dangerous place, unsafe for fragile flesh and blood?

Eventually, Tess found a door in a corner of the yard that led us to the Gadgetorium. There, in the midst of the improbable gadgets on display, the prize feature was Dr. Gatling's Lunar Dismembulator Cannon. The text on a plaque beside it explained: "Mounted in the center of a dirigible cap, the cannon fires plasma balls and is capable of defending the airship from sky pirates and menacing flying creatures..."

Tess took my hand once more and dragged me around the corner, out of the gloomy Gadgetorium and into the gift shop. Had this really been just a museum? I blinked. Teresa smiled at me. What was she saying? She wanted to buy some souvenir Steampunk glasses and a hat?

The Oamaru Steampunk Museum is one of a kind. It also serves as the World Steampunk Headquarters. Steampunk, for those who don't know, is a genre of science fiction that takes its cue from Victorian-age authors such as Jules Verne and H.G. Wells, who wrote novels about yet-to-be-invented technologies based on the science of the day — much of it powered by steam, but extending to fantastical devices like submarines, spaceships, and time machines. This imagined Victorian future of the past is the world of Steampunk. The "punk" part is the edgy, nonconformist attitude the writers, artists, gamers, musicians, and others devoted to the genre bring to it. For example, the British sci-fi TV show *Dr Who* has strong elements of Steampunk in it.

Tess Torridon and her hapless partner, geared up for adventure in the Gadgetorium. We may never take off our futuristic-Victorian top hats and goggles.

Steampunk came and went as a fad about a decade ago, but the aesthetic captivated some people, including Iain Clark, who launched the Steampunk Festival in Oamaru in 2010. Clark, who likes to be known as "Agent Darling," later established the museum and the World Headquarters (honestly, there may not have been that much competition for the latter).

The festival has spawned a local market specializing in Steampunk chic, with shops selling top hats, waistcoats, corsets, boots, jewelry, the all-important goggles (for traveling fast in futuristic steam-powered machines), and other paraphernalia. There's a dedicated Steampunk arcade located in an old warehouse near the museum. But the vibe leaks out. Throughout town I spied a bit of Steampunk here and there. For instance, there's a stray mechanical boar rooting around near the Toyota dealership. I can only imagine it must have escaped from the museum's menagerie.

In front of Steampunk World HQ

But why *this* small port town on the Pacific coast of New Zealand's South Island? Does the town straddle cosmic wormholes? No. But it has the best-preserved Victorian-era architecture in New Zealand.

This part of New Zealand has lots of relatively flat and fertile land suitable for farming. And so, in the 1850s and 1860s, as British settlement expanded in the South Island, Oamuru village grew into a major exporter of wheat and wool. As the harbor's shipping trade grew, warehouses were built, then hotels, bars, brothels — even banks. Since trees were scarce in this region, most of the construction was with large blocks of the abundantly available local limestone. Then came the gold rush. The town boomed. They built impressive neoclassical edifices — pillars and all — along the length of Thames Street. By the 1880s, Oamaru was the size of San Francisco.

The boom years were followed by several decades of bust. Companies that had borrowed heavily to finance grand offices went broke. Just as the town once flourished, so now it withered. Limestone, however, does not decay like human fortunes. In one way Oamaru was lucky: it had no earthquakes, fires, or floods. Lacking the impetus for modern development, the stone buildings were never replaced by glass and steel. By late in the twentieth century, the citizens discovered they were living in a miraculously preserved Victorian-era town. Suddenly, the old buildings were historic, and this began to draw the tourists.

Although Oamaru has never recovered its glory days, tourism has brought it a second life. There is also an annual Victorian Heritage Festival in town, with shops that dress and cater to the traditionalists. Teresa and I sauntered into a Victorian clothing shop which must have had more than 200 dresses on the racks, as well as in-costume staff ready to help. I made the mistake of saying to one woman that I imagined many of the Steampunk crowd would also come here for rentals during their festival. There was a sharp intake of breath. Had she been wearing her pearls, she would have clutched them. She explained in rather severe tones that these costumes were for *Victorian* make-believe only!

I like to imagine a relentless but genteel feud being waged in the shadows of these limestone edifices between the Steampunks and the Victorians, like the Crips and the Bloods: the future-fantasists and historical-traditionalists each staking out their turf and their timeline in Oamaru.

But mostly, I just loved the sheer fantasy fun of it all (see page C19).

Chapter 23

Geological Oddballs: The Moeraki Boulders

Giant's Gobstoppers. Alien Eggs. New Zealand's Stonehenge. These are just some of the names that have been applied to one of the most improbable-looking geological oddities in all of New Zealand, the Moeraki Boulders. To the Māori, they were ancient eel baskets, thrown overboard when a great canoe of the ancestors capsized. The canoe became a large offshore reef; the boulders, half buried in the sand, looked like inverted giant baskets, turned to stone. I smiled at the myth when I first heard it. But when I saw the Moeraki Boulders with my own eyes, some of them 2 meters (6 feet) wide and almost perfectly spherical — damn, I could not come up with a better explanation.

Teresa and I stopped for a gander at the boulders as we were driving from Oamaru to central Otago, and we saw the signpost to the beach. We thought, sure, this will be a little amusing. After trudging along the sand for a while, when we finally came upon them, they stopped us dead in our tracks. It was hard to make sense of what we were seeing. What forces of nature can make a boulder perfectly spherical?

Pick one of these explanations, or think up something of your own:

1. Lumps of molten lava were thrown up by volcanoes. They spun in the air into perfect spheres, then hardened before they hit the ground.
2. Large rocks were picked up by glaciers and deposited on the beach, where waves and sand rolled them for millions of years, like a rock tumbler, until they were round.

3. Bits of sediment accumulated around something sticky, and over time added layers and layers, like a pearl in an oyster growing from a grain of sand.
4. The boulders are fossilized giant jellyfish.

Left: Upturned ancient eel baskets? Right: Alien eggs?

The answer is number 3. The Moeraki Boulders are what's known as *concretizations*, and they are formed in a similar manner to a pearl. Just as an oyster coats an irritating grain of sand with layers of nacre to form a pearl, so concretization forms when a speck of something "sticky" — a small pebble or shell — finds its way into sediment that has not yet hardened. Minerals in the sediment, such as calcite (a key mineral in making concrete), attach all around the suspended speck, forming layer after layer of encapsulating material that hardens even as the surrounding sediment stays as soft as gelatinous mud, like giant gumballs suspended in jelly.

This process took place in a shallow coastal sea some 60 million years ago. When the land rose, the sediment dried and hardened into sandstone. The waves wore down the sandstone and scoured out the hard concretizations onto the shore. Teresa and I found a couple of boulders still partly buried where the cliff meets the beach. Who knows how many more boulders are still embedded within the cliffs, ready to roll out and onto the shore as the oceans rise in the decades to come?

Tim plays Sisyphus with a Moeraki Boulder still partially embedded in the cliff.

What I enjoyed most about the Moeraki Boulders was simply encountering something inexplicable, and then learning that science can in fact explain how it came to be. Of course, there's much more we still don't know about the forces that forged the world we live in — a world of wonders we too often walk through with our eyes half closed.

Chapter 24

Of Gold and Grapes in the Otago Valley

Gold: how it has shaped our world!

From the Otago Peninsula, Teresa and I traveled into the vast emptiness of central Otago, towards Bannockburn, a little village in the Otago Valley just an hour east of Queenstown. We were headed there because we simply had not had enough of Otago wineries, and there are *133* of them.

The journey through central Otago was like driving through Wyoming: endless valleys of winter-blond grass and grizzled, scrub-covered hills with snow on the tops of them. A cold wind was blowing. The settlements here are few and far between: small and rough sheep-farming towns that have only dwindled in size since the days of the gold rush.

The Otago gold rush of the 1860s was the biggest in New Zealand. Some 18,000 men hoping to strike it rich flooded the interior. They came inland from along the coast, but also from overseas, from England, Scotland, California, even China. It took them weeks of travel along the mud roads with horses and wagons. When they arrived at one of Otago's 80 different gold fields, they pitched their tents, sorted out their supplies and whatever claim they had staked, then got to work.

I had my own naive notions about what gold mining must have been like: washing and sifting gravel from a riverbed with a tin pan with holes in the bottom, then plucking out the nuggets. But that of course is not how one seriously searches for alluvial gold. The reality is, you have to break up a mountain into tiny bits first. What does it look like, when two thousand gold-hungry men set about sifting through a single mountainside? At Bannockburn, it looks like this:

A small section of the Bannockburn Sluicings

The clifftop to the left of the valley (above) was "ground level" of what was once a smooth hillside of the Carrick Mountain Range called the "Carrick Fan." All the land beneath the cliff was mined away in just five years or so during the search for gold — and this is only a small part of the "Bannockburn Sluicings" (see page C19).

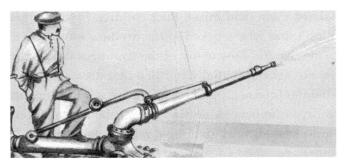

Artwork of a hydraulic hose, from one of several plaques on the site that explain how miners broke down the hillsides in search of gold

The challenge for the gold hunters was that the geological forces that formed these hills deposited most of the gold in a layer between gravels and sediments. The miners couldn't simply tunnel in; they had to wash away whole hillsides with hydraulic hoses to get at the gravel, and then painstakingly sift through it for the heavier particles of gold.

To run the hoses, they needed plenty of water. This was one of the big challenges of mining in Bannockburn, for the area is in the "rain shadow" of the Southern Alps. In fact, when Teresa and I drove into Bannockburn, we passed a road sign that read "Welcome to the Desert." A few streams ran through the valley, but not enough to meet the miners' demand. Rock channels were built through the sluicings to direct water from the mountains into reservoirs that could feed the hoses. On my hike, I found the remains of one of these reservoirs, together with a sign that explained how the two brothers who built it made their fortunes not by mining, but, cleverly, by selling the water from their reservoir to the miners.

It was weird to walk through this man-made canyon. It was so beautiful, and yet so ugly to think of this land literally ripped apart just to get at the gold. The various history museums Teresa and I had visited around the South Island made it clear that gold mining was a hard life for the miners, and for the women who married them (and raised their children in the camps), not to mention those who worked in the brothels in mining towns. It made me wonder how many of the countless thousands who came here to get rich actually fulfilled that dream.

I sifted the Internet, panning for answers, but came up with no definitive numbers. A Radio New Zealand show about the Otago gold rush did say that most miners never struck it rich. Many others perished en route to the gold fields. And the ones who did find gold? Well, according to the show, many had dreams of buying their own farm, while others had failed in business and, destitute, came to the gold fields because there was no better option. Those who found gold spent their money as you might expect: "They dressed like pirates in high boots, tight velvet trousers and loose shirts — often dyed red, pale yellow or blue. They accessorised with silk, sashes, gold rings and watch chains..."

The radio show also explained that while miners came to Otago from Europe and North America, many Māori were also miners; they often worked in tribal units, not as individual prospectors. Thousands more came from China, resulting in a rise in anti-Chinese prejudice among the New Zealanders of European descent.

All told, the Otago gold rush was the richest in New Zealand, yielding some 195 tons (175 tonnes). That's about twice as much gold as the famous Klondike gold rush. Walking through this ruined hillside, it's easy to question whether or not it was worth it. But the real impact of gold for New Zealand was not in the metal extracted. Gold opened up the interior of the country, built towns, communities, schools. It created a dynamic economy in the coastal cities that supplied the miners, and those cities — Dunedin, Invercargill — are still thriving in the twenty-first century, without any dependence on gold.

It surprised me to learn there is still one gold mine operating in the Bannockburn area. There was some gold left in the ground after the boom subsided and the miners moved on. But what remained was hard to wrest from the rock until modern methods were developed in the early twentieth century. These basically involved crushing massive amounts of raw ore and then bathing it in cyanide to leach out molecules of gold. Such a mine processes hundreds of tons of raw rock a day to extract about an ounce-and-a-half (40 grams) of gold per ton. It costs roughly 75% as much to produce the gold as the value of the gold itself. The Bannockburn mine went bankrupt in the 1990s but has been bought by an Australian firm that plans to restart it when the price of gold gets high enough.

For now, grapes are the new gold in Otago, and indeed, the current rush to sluice the juice reminds me of the gold-rush days. Otago is the furthest-south wine region in the entire world. So many small wineries have sprung up on these dry hills, they have changed the landscape in their own way. Teresa and I wanted to visit some of these wineries, but with 133 to choose from, we didn't have a clue where to start. Luckily, our B&B owner had worked as a wine agent, and she recommended a few outstanding wineries to us.

The first one we visited, Domaine Thomson, is owned by the great-great-grandson of John Turnbull Thomson, known as "Surveyor Thomson." Thomson explored and mapped central Otago in the 1850s. He was also a painter, and the walls of the winery's tasting room are adorned with his works that show what the region looked like in the decades before gold, and the mad rush that transformed the land. The human figures in his landscapes are drawn in the middle distance, so that they appear so tiny, one fears they could easily get lost in those endless hills, with the snow-capped ragged mountains far behind them. One painting (below) particularly caught my eye: The men and their pack animals have stopped; their backs are to the viewer, their faces towards the mountains. One feels *their* sense of this vastness — before roads, before way-stations, before smartphones. They are walking into the unknown. But there is gold somewhere in this abyss, and so onward they walk…

Domaine Thomson's wines were the best we tasted in Otago. Pinot Noir grapes, the region's specialty, love a dry climate, and the schist-filled soil gives the resulting wine a distinct earthy flavor you won't find in France or California. I asked the friendly fellow who poured our glasses in the tasting room what it takes for a winery to stand out in Otago when there is so much competition. "A good winemaker," he replied. There are a few in the region who move about from winery to winery, and they tend to win the gold medals for the wineries they work for.

John Turnbull Thomson's orginal art, displayed in Domaine Thomson's tasting room (used with permission)

Maybe it's just my prejudice, but wineries seem a much more palatable way for humans to live on the land. Extracting a good vintage requires care for the soil and the environment, whereas crushing tons of rock and soaking it in cyanide to extract gold — *doesn't*. I'd rather discover a gold-medal Pinot than a piece of gold metal any day.

Chapter 25

Snowed In at Aoraki/Mount Cook

Heavy snow was forecast on the day we drove to Aoraki/Mount Cook. I've driven through plenty of snowstorms in my native Canada. But in New Zealand, they tend to close the roads when it snows. With no other accommodation nearby, if they shut the one road to the mountain, Teresa and I would be out in the cold.

When we reached the shores of Lake Pūkaki, the sky was still bright blue, almost as blue as the lake itself. Lake Pūkaki is glacier-fed. The glacial silt contains fine mineral particles that, suspended in water, reflect the sunlight, turning the lake a brilliant turquoise, Miami-Beach blue. The lake appears to glow.

As we drove along the water's edge towards the mountains, we could see the storm brewing. It was a spectacular sight. New Zealand's Southern Alps rise up, north to south, creating a wall of rock that is 3 kilometers (nearly 2 miles) high in places. The ferocious, moist winds that swirl around the sub-Antarctic regions blow in from the west, then slam into that massive rock wall, forcing the air up to the peaks. It cools rapidly, condensing into rain on the west coast, and snow higher up, where it spills over the peaks like a giant atmospheric waterfall. Snow deluges the eastern sides of the mountains, but leaves the land further east in the "rain shadow." It is one of the driest parts of all New Zealand.

We could see that waterfall of snow straight ahead of us, and we were driving right into it. By the time we arrived at the little village of Aoraki/Mount Cook at the entrance to the National Park, big white gobs were falling like cornflakes, leaving huge, melting splotches on our windshield as we searched for the charging station for our EV. A few hours later, the highways department closed the road.

The road to Aoraki/Mount Cook. Note the atmospheric waterfall in the distance.

We stayed at the Hermitage Hotel — or rather, the third reconstruction of the original Hermitage. It was built in 1884 for the first tourists drawn to New Zealand's highest peak. Aoraki/Mount Cook has been attracting hikers and mountain climbers since climbing became a sport. Sir Edmund Hillary trained here, in preparation for his first ascent of Mount Everest, and so there's a climbing museum attached to the hotel, named in his honor.

It snowed all the next day, so the road stayed closed, creating havoc for tourists on a tight schedule. But not for us. We snuggled in and enjoyed the whiteout. The hotel is brilliantly built so that every room has a view of the peak of Aoraki/Mount Cook. Teresa, naturally, had convinced me to get a premium-deluxe room on the ninth floor for the best view possible. Next morning the view from our premium-deluxe floor-to-ceiling window looked like a display of gray cotton batten. There was no mountain peak to be seen at all.

Mountain attire from the local Department of Conservation museum. Left to right: Pre-European Māori forager; Victorian-era climber; modern search-and-rescue volunteer

About a foot of snow was on the ground, and our little Polestar was buried so deep I had to shovel it out. After breakfast, the hotel lobby was packed with people and luggage. They had checked out, but there was nowhere to go. They were rescheduling flights and negotiating deals to extend their stay — including an entire wedding party.

Teresa and I lounged about by the fire, watching the chaos swirl around us, then decided to explore the museum, which featured a terrifying movie about the volunteer mountain rescue teams who put their own lives in danger to save unlucky climbers. Because the weather can change so quickly, and the ice and snow ridges are so unstable, Aoraki/Mount Cook has claimed a lot of mountaineers' lives over the years. More than 240 have died on its slopes. A Nepali Sherpa who was a guide on Aoraki/Mount Cook for 20 years said it was as dangerous as climbing Everest.

Left: The Hermitage Hotel, a black oblong slab in the distance, as seen on my hike to Hooker Lake. Right: A frigid bride, bouquet in hand, poses in the snow in front of the hotel.

The Department of Conservation also had a display in its own separate info center, which included an explanation of the rather awkward name for the mountain. *Aoraki* is the Māori name for the peak. According to legend, Aoraki was the eldest son of the sky god. Together with his brothers, Aoraki piloted a giant canoe from the heavens to the earth to visit his mother, the earth goddess. At a crucial moment, Aoraki's canoe capsized. Aoraki and his brothers climbed to the top of the boat, and there they turned to stone. The canoe became the whole South Island, and the brothers became the five greatest peaks of the Southern Alps, with Aoraki the tallest among them.

The story behind the English name for the mountain seems utterly prosaic in comparison: In 1851 Captain J.L. Stokes sighted the peak while sailing along the west coast, and named it in honor of the English "discoverer" of New Zealand, Captain James Cook. Up until 1998, descendants of the colonizers only referred to the mountain as "Mount Cook." But in 1998, following a massive land settlement between the Crown and South Island Māori, a number of South Island place names were amended to include their original Māori names. Aoraki/Mount Cook is especially significant among these changes, because it is the only place where the Māori name legally precedes the English.

By the afternoon of our third day, the weather, though still overcast, had improved enough that I headed out on one of the more ambitious hikes to the base of Aoraki/Mount Cook. Although over a foot of fresh snow had fallen, the trail had been cleared by park staff with a small snow-blower, making the hiking easy, if a bit slippery. The dark green-gray vegetation beneath the thick duvet of snow turned the entire valley into a sepia-tone photograph.

The trail rose to a viewpoint of a small glacial lake, Lake Mueller, which was covered by a thin sheet of slate-blue ice. The remnants of glaciers clung to the mountainsides. Every now and then I heard a rumble like thunder — an avalanche. I counted four of them in the space of half an hour, way up near the glaciers. Further along, a suspension bridge crossed a small river, its jade waters flowing between white-topped black boulders. I felt as if I had entered Narnia during the perpetual winter of the Ice Queen (see page C20).

For all its remoteness, this trail was remarkably crowded. There must have been a hundred people out that afternoon. Of course, everyone had been cooped up in the hotel for days, and this hike was reputed as one of the best in all of New Zealand — because of its brilliant views of Aoraki/Mount Cook, which remained shrouded in cloud the whole day.

Some of the other hikers seem quite underdressed. For example: young Chinese women in tennis shoes and pretty skirts; they were clearly prioritizing their Instagram selfies over prevention of frostbite. At the other end of the fashion spectrum, I passed burly Australian men (they looked like rugby players) wearing only shorts and jerseys. Perhaps that's all they had packed?

As foot traffic ran both ways along the trench-like trail, whenever two groups needed to pass, one had to stand aside in the much deeper snow. These cross-cultural encounters were managed with surprising civility and courtesy, although in one case, as I moved aside for a young Japanese woman, she also moved aside for me — and stepped right off the edge of a low walkway into waist-deep snow! Her friends and I hauled her back onto her feet, with much embarrassed giggling and bowing. It was a good warning, though. Had the slope been much steeper and the snow deeper, she could have sunk right out of our sight.

Four suspension-bridge crossings later, and 90 minutes after the start, I arrived at the endpoint of the trail: Hooker Lake, with a great view of the Hooker Glacier at the far end of it, just a tiny remnant of the once massive river of ice that a few hundred years ago filled the valley and flowed from the base of Aoraki/Mount Cook to the plains; Hooker Lake is but a puddle of tears left by its retreat. About a dozen hikers huddled around a few picnic tables. Selfies were snapped, and people rubbed their bare hands. It was too cold to linger. Somewhere above in the clouds, the frozen face of the god Aoraki loomed over us.

On the walk back to the Hermitage, I could see down the valley to distant Lake Pūkaki. It was shocking to see that the land around the lake was beige, not white. No snow at all had fallen on the dry grasses in the "rain shadow" beyond the mountains.

The final morning of our stay in the Hermitage, we woke up to blue sky. The sun was not yet visible, but it reflected hot-pink light off the white peak of Aoraki/Mount Cook. Ah... so this is what all the fuss is about (see below)!

Leaving the mountains on such a sunny day was not easy. Yet, as we drove back along Lake Pūkaki, we noticed something strange. The further away from Aoraki/Mount Cook we got, the larger the mountain seemed to grow. How was this possible? I imagined that from the Hermitage, surrounded by other, closer peaks, we couldn't get the proper sense of how much higher Aoraki/Mount Cook really is (see page C20). Barely 15 minutes down the road, when we looked back it was hard to believe we had actually lived there for three days, at the foot of — oh, I can't stand it any longer... Let's do away altogether with this silly British usurpation of the original Māori names — at the foot of *Aoraki*, the great frozen son of the sky god and the earth goddess.

This is the view of Aoraki from our window on the last morning.

Chapter 26

The Brightest Stars in the Darkest Sky: Lake Tekapo

Have you ever wondered what the stars look like in the darkest sky in the world? I just found out.

We left Aoraki/Mount Cook on a bright winter's day in mid-August. Sunlight bounced off the glacial waters of Lake Pūkaki as we drove south along its shoreline, reflecting the light as a deep turquoise hue. Teresa and I were only traveling 90 minutes down the road to the next glacial lake, Lake Tekapo, in Mackenzie County. This 'high country' of New Zealand's South Island is known to the local Māori iwi, the Ngāti Tahu, as the "Hole in the Middle."

We stopped along the way at a stunning viewpoint at the end of Lake Pūkaki that featured a Māori pavilion which explained the region's curious moniker. According to the display, in 1848 the Ngāti Tahu iwi sold 14 million acres of plains land to the New Zealand government. The tribe intended that the boundary would be the foothills of the mountains. However, the government assumed control of *all* the land from the foothills right up to the Southern Alps. Many Ngāti Tahu found themselves suddenly landless. And when tribe members traveled to their traditional resource camps for summer hunting and fishing, they were suddenly treated as trespassers.

In 1877, over 100 Ngāti Tahu members staged a peaceful protest over the injustice of the "Hole in the Middle," camping out on their traditional land until they were forcibly removed two years later. The dispute has never been resolved, but work is underway to address it right now. In recent years the government has agreed to renegotiate areas of historical-cultural value for the iwi, and so an extensive cultural-mapping project has begun that will build a Ngāti Tahu atlas. This will establish a historical-cultural claim for their case of ownership.

One of the biggest upsides of restoring tribal ownership of the "Hole in the Middle" is that the Māori have always seen themselves as custodians of the land. "People perish, but land is permanent," is a Māori saying I have come across several times. The government has made many deals with the Māori in the past several years to return their stolen lands under the aegis of joint conservation stewardship. To me, this is an exciting way forward for the country. It also marks a change of direction for the Pākehā population, after 150 years of committing treaty violations and ecological damage. It's the rare case where one right can correct two wrongs.

The natural value of the "Hole in the Middle" is simply that it is pretty much a hole: empty of most human development. It's a harsh, dry landscape, and one of the last places in New Zealand to be converted into pasture. It is also stunningly beautiful. Driving in along State Highway 8 towards Lake Tekapo in wintertime is visually overwhelming: the turquoise lake is ringed on three sides by rough, tan hills covered in fresh white snow. It's a palette of perfect colors. It makes me wish I were a painter, simply to have the excuse to stand by this stark shore, brush in hand, and gaze across the water for hours (see page C21).

The first European to arrive at Lake Tekapo was a Scotsman, James Mackenzie. In 1855, Mackenzie and his dog, Friday, drove a flock of stolen sheep into this high country, sure that no one would ever find them way up here. The law caught up with Mackenzie, eventually. However, catching him proved easier that rounding up his stolen sheep, scattered in the hills. History is funny, though. Mackenzie the sheep stealer has been immortalized: this whole area is called Mackenzie Country. There's also the Mackenzie District, the Mackenzie Basin, and the Mackenzie Mountains. Meanwhile, the men who pursued the outlaw in the name of justice are long forgotten.

Lake Tekapo

Legal sheep ranching in the high country followed soon after Mackenzie's arrest. But it was hard going. Only large leaseholds of several thousand acres were big enough to support profitable herds. Several bitter winters in the late 1800s killed many sheep. Today, it's still a tough business, as wool prices have declined globally. The government removed some farm subsidies in the 1990s, and now reviews leaseholds to make sure they are complying with what some farmers see as excessive environmental regulations.

Farmers make the case that they do a better job of caring for the land than the government does on areas it has set aside for conservation. The latter get overrun with invasive species and pests like wilding pines, rabbits, and wallabies (introduced from Australia), which farmers work vigilantly to reduce on the land they control.

As ranchers struggle to hang on, citizens of the little town of Tekapo look to tourism and science for their economic future. The draw: Tekapo's dark night sky. Why is the sky so dark? Because there is no light beneath it. To the north, east, and south the nearest population centers are more than 150 kilometers (90 miles) distant. Looking to the west, there is nothing but sheep farms between Tekapo and the coast of Australia, some 4000 km (2500 miles) away. As a result, this whole region has been declared the "Aoraki Mackenzie International Dark Sky Reserve." It is the largest gold-standard International Dark Sky Reserve in the world.

And so, the "Hole in the Middle" has become a window to the heavens.

Observatory at the peak of Mount John, Tekapo

Right next to Tekapo is a little mountain, Mount John. On its peak, four world-class telescope observatories and a dozen other instruments have been erected by the University of Canterbury.

Its astronomy department conducts research projects on Mount John, as well as sharing the facilities with other astronomers from around the world.

The enterprising Dark Sky Experience Company, in partnership with the university and Ngāi Tahu Tourism, have set up a cluster of activities that take a hundred or so tourists each night to Mount John to watch the heavens through their telescopes. It gives them the best view of the southern sky in the world. The company center in Tekapo includes a beautiful display about Māori astronomy and the legends of the ancestors contained within traditional Māori constellations.

The Dark Sky tours are so popular that they were sold out for all but one night during the four days Teresa and I stayed in Tekapo. Unfortunately, the night we were due to go, cloud cover had rolled in and the tour was canceled. But we didn't mind so much. Just stepping outside our door on a moonless night was all we needed.

The Milky Way arched above us so brightly it looked as if we were seeing it from outer space. I'm fortunate to have seen the Milky Way from Canada's far north. But the view from Tekapo was even clearer. I could see with my naked eye thousands of individual, roughly spherical, three-dimensional shapes that were distant stars, or clusters of stars, within our galaxy. It was less like a milky way and more like celestial bubble tea, with tiny globes of light suspended in the black bowl of night. I could sense the depth, the *spaciousness* of space.

I craned my neck till it hurt from looking up. I felt as if I could fall into the cosmos. Why was gravity holding my feet to the ground, I wondered? That seemed so ridiculous, when there was so much infinity drawing me skyward.

The Dark Sky Reserve Project points to humanity's global addiction to light, showing that the cost of this addiction is the loss of the night sky. Their website sums up their vision and their purpose:

Millions of children across the world will never see a star, let alone appreciate the Milky Way. We believe that, together, we can change this. The night sky should be accessible to everyone on the planet — tonight, tomorrow and into the future.

I'd never thought about this before. I've worked with many development experts at the World Bank for whom rural electrification, including street lighting, is taken for granted as a universal good. Kids can study at night, and working late is safer for those who would otherwise walk home in the dark. Economists study satellite images of the Earth at night in order to correlate the illumination of countries with their level of economic development. More light at night has been an *unquestioned* marker of progress. But how do we quantify the cost of the loss of the dark night sky culturally, psychologically, *spiritually*? We don't.

The Dark Sky Reserve Project recommends that corporations shut off their lights and that residents close their curtains at night. In places like Tekapo, these measures have become local bylaws, simply because the town has realized the darkness is good for business. Even so, as tourism has boomed in Tekapo, new hotels have been built. The lights of one of them shone visibly into our backyard, so that we had to shield our eyes from that direction as we scanned the stars. Air B&Bs have also proliferated. Tourists in the new digs don't always follow the rules about keeping their curtains shut at night. There seems to be no enforcement for the local dark-sky bylaws. Will Tekapo be able to expand much further without tainting the very night sky that is the reason the town is thriving? Or will town officials succeed — in a good way — in keeping its citizens in the dark?

Imagine, if you will, a world in which the night sky is dark everywhere, a world in which the cosmos shines bright in all our lives each and every evening. How would it change us, as a species, if all we needed to do was look up to be reminded of our humble place in the universe, and to lose our tiny selves, with all our cares, in the infinity of space?

Chapter 27

After the Quake: Christchurch Resurrected

After ten days in New Zealand's spectacular and wild Southern Alps, Teresa and I headed for Christchurch, the second-largest city in New Zealand (population 390,000). As we descended from the mountains towards the Canterbury Plains and the coast, we felt our spirits sag.

I have to confess, New Zealand's cities have left us underwhelmed. Auckland, Wellington, and Dunedin lack the historic architecture of pretty much any city in Europe. That's not really surprising, considering the indigenous Māori built their settlements out of wood, which decays quickly in the humid climate, and the first colonists didn't arrive until the 1820s. Earthquakes, floods, and fires, plus indiscriminate development, have destroyed much of what was even slightly old. But the modern buildings (with a handful of exceptions) don't feel particularly inspiring either. As flâneurs, we seek the city's streets to learn its story. Sadly, it seems urban New Zealand doesn't have much to say.

So imagine our surprise: we liked Christchurch! It's not as if the buildings had been designed by Christoper Wren or Antoni Gaudi. But the city has an energy about it, a dynamism, a vibe. This is all the more strange because the city was utterly devastated by two back-to-back earthquakes in 2010 and 2011.

Our hotel was easy walking distance from the center of town, and just a few blocks away from Quake City, the earthquake museum, which is where our exploration started. The story was grim: almost 200 people were killed in the quakes, and about 80% of the downtown buildings were destroyed or badly damaged. Thousands lost their homes. One whole eastern section of the city has been condemned forever: no one is allowed to resume living there because the ground there liquefied during the quake; there's no safe way to rebuild on the mud.

Walking around the downtown core, we could see at a glance that many buildings are still under reconstruction. The Christchurch Cathedral lost its bell tower, and remains shrouded in scaffolding; the city museum was destroyed. We saw one large, modern apartment complex on prime real-estate that remained empty. Perhaps it was not safe enough to restore, but too expensive to demolish? Its bottom floor was covered with graffiti.

And yet, at the heart of the city center, we found a renovated restaurant-and-shopping area that bustled with activity and buzzed with the conversation of a thousand diners out on the terraces at lunchtime. A beautiful river ran right next to the cafés, with gardens and parks all along both banks. This was the Ōtākaro Avon River. The little watercourse was pristine, clear as diamonds, as it flowed from its glacial source through the city center, and then on through the suburbs to the ocean. The water was not always this pure; the whole watercourse is being brought back to life thanks to the government's post-earthquake River Regeneration Plan.

A river runs through it: the Ōtākaro Avon River alongside Christchurch's new restaurant district

One afternoon I did an urban hike along the riverwalk. Near the quaint punting boathouse, I was astounded to discover dozens of large eels as long as my arm slithering in the water around the dock. These creatures were once an important food source for the Māori. How cool that the river is now clean enough that they have returned.

Although the history museum was still closed for repairs, the art museum was open. The building is itself a work of art; the façade is a wave of undulating glass panes that seems in motion as the clouds pass, reflected in the glass. Built before the earthquake, the art museum miraculously suffered only a few broken panels during the disaster. I can honestly say, I think it is the most creative building I've seen in all of New Zealand (see page C22).

On the side wall of the museum, in large neon lights, a clear message shines forth for the citizens still shaken by the quake: "Everything is going to be alright." I imagine passersby looking up, consciously or unconsciously reading the sign, and then finding themselves humming a familiar reggae tune, and feeling strangely reassured, their burdens suddenly resting a little lighter on their shoulders.

Outside the small downtown core, Christchurch is mostly one-story homes and small businesses. This low profile must have helped a lot during the quake. But it also gives the city a homey, small-town neighborhood vibe. It's hard to explain it, but to me lots of New Zealand suburbs look like bland, soulless wastelands. Not Christchurch. Christchurch feels like a collection of cozy communities.

I asked Teresa how she felt about this. She told me, "Christchurch feels like a city where people have a voice in its future. It's not a town being redesigned by city planners and developers in some back room. It feels like a town where people have a say in the kind of place their children will grow up in."

Perhaps my favorite place in the whole city was the old Botanic Garden, which was just a few blocks from our hotel. Founded in 1863, the park initially served as a testing ground for introducing English plants and crops to New Zealand, to see how well they could adapt to the new colony. It has grown considerably in size and scope since then.

At the heart of the park I found the New Zealand Icons Garden. Hundreds of native species from across the islands have been planted here in a re-creation of various New Zealand ecosystems. Walking through these lush landscapes took me back to some of my favorite hikes from all across the country: one minute in a subtropical rainforest full of ferns, the next in a wetland pond filled with ducks, then among giant blue succulents in arid scrubland. It felt like I was strolling through a "greatest hits" album of New Zealand wildernesses.

While all this foliage was a veritable world of verdant wonders, the most astounding tree in the whole park was separated from the rest. It was a small, spindly-looking tree with drooping, fern-like leaves. Not much to look at, really. Kind of like a Charlie-Brown-pathetic-Christmas tree, compared to the others. It was encased in a circular metal fence, as if it might try to pick up its roots and run away!

This was, in fact, one of the rarest trees in the entire world — a living fossil. The Wollemi pine was thought to be extinct for many millions of years, its fossils dating back 90 million years. Then in 1994 an Australian park ranger named David Noble stumbled across a cluster of them growing in a remote canyon in the rainforests of the Blue Mountains in New South Wales. There are believed to be fewer than 100 Wollemi pines left in the wild.

To mark the 150th anniversary of the Botanic Garden, a Wollemi pine was transplanted here as part of the effort to increase the odds of this botanical dinosaur's survival. As we have all learned from watching *Jurassic Park* movies, one has to be careful when introducing prehistoric life-forms to the modern world. For this reason, rather than planting a seed, this tree was grown from sample tissue to avoid any inadvertent introduction of diseases that might have clung to an actual seed from the native forest.

Wollemi pine: dinosaur tree

The Wollemi pine is the first tree for a new section of the park called Gondwana Garden, named after the ancient, vast southern supercontinent that once consisted of what is now New Zealand, Australia, Antarctica, Africa, South America, and India. The goal will be to populate Gondwana Garden with other survivors of this long-gone world. And who knows, maybe clone some dinosaurs from DNA extracted from prehistoric mosquitoes trapped in amber? What could possibly go wrong?

Near the end of our Christchurch stay, I discovered that there was a temporary location of the history museum that was open while the old building underwent repairs. The museum featured a striking special exhibit called "Six Extinctions." The exhibit explained the five previous mass extinctions on planet Earth, illustrated with fossils and models — plus the sixth, which we are slow-rolling towards right now due to human-driven habitat loss, overexploitation of natural resources, and climate change.

To me it seemed rather "in your face" for the museum to launch an exhibit on extinctions in a city recently devastated by an earthquake. But I liked the *ballsyness* of it. I've come to see New Zealanders as an excessively safety-conscious lot — so many traffic cones! I think the museum has a better approach: look your existential threats right in the eye.

It made me think about just how poorly most cities prepare their citizens for disasters. In the US every year, one city or another on the eastern seaboard gets clobbered by a severe hurricane. Floods devastated New Hampshire and the Northeast recently. Massive wildfires in California and Canada have killed dozens, and made the air unsafe for hundreds of millions more. Phoenix, Arizona, had 54 days of 110 degree Fahrenheit heat (43 °C) in a row in the summer of 2023, with 194 confirmed heat-related deaths by early September. And yet most North Americans react as if each incident is a freak accident. Who could have seen it coming?

Maybe Christchurch's recent earthquakes have shaken the city out of its complacency, and that, ultimately, is a positive thing? The history museum's extinction exhibit is right across the street from the art museum's neon sign, "Everything is going to be alright." So which is it? I am probably expecting too much to believe this is a deliberate tension created between the two institutions. But if that were the case, I would applaud Christchurch for fostering that tension in its citizens, for it will build their psychological resilience for disasters yet to come. And we are all going to need that kind of resilience, aren't we?

Chapter 28

Akaroa: French New Zealand

Just south of Christchurch, which is as flat as a mat, the land rises in a dramatic forest-covered ridge like a great, green wall. On the other side of that wall is the Banks Peninsula, which sticks out into the South Pacific and resembles a giant wrinkled toe, covered in grass — all 440 square miles (1100 sq. km) of it. The roughly oval shape of this mountainous area reveals its origin as the cones of two contiguous volcanoes which erupted between 11 and 8 million years ago. Eons of rising and falling sea levels, wind, and rain sculpted these cones as if on the wheel of a divine potter — a potter with violent tendencies, who every now and then dashed the cones to the floor, leaving them cracked and broken apart, yet strangely all the more beautiful for the apparent violence done to them. The center of each cone is now a dramatic harbor, surrounded by rugged hills but for a single outlet to the ocean.

On the shore of the largest of these two craters rests the little village of Akaroa, the first permanent European settlement on the peninsula. Remarkably, it was founded not by the British, but by the French.

Incroyable! Mais, comment est-ce arrivé? — I hear you ask, in your perfectly accented French. Okay, I'll tell you the story of how it happened.

In 1838, Jean François Langlois, a French whaling-ship captain, obtained a deed of purchase for the entire Banks Peninsula from a dozen Māori chiefs (£6 paid in advance, with the balance of £234 due in commodities later). He sailed back to France, document in hand, and began recruiting settlers for what was to be not just a simple support settlement for French whalers, but also the first French colony in New Zealand — a strategic step towards the French government's grand vision of colonizing the South Pacific.

Two years later, when Langlois returned on the ship *Comte de Paris* with a boatload of brave French settlers, he was greeted by the British Union Jack flying in Akaroa Harbor. In 1840, Britain had signed the Waitangi Treaty with over 500 Māori chiefs, and New Zealand had become a British colony. The Brits knew the French were coming, and they made jolly-well sure to have the flag waving when the newcomers made land.

Akaroa harbor, at the center of the other volcano on Banks Peninsula, with Akaroa village on the far shore. The summit route runs all along the curved ridge that was the rim of the crater.

However, the British allowed the crestfallen immigrants to settle and build their new homes at Akaroa while the thorny legal issue of land ownership was resolved. To complicate matters for Langlois, it turned out his deed had not been signed by a majority of the chiefs whose tribes inhabited the peninsula — including tribes he never even knew existed. In the end, rather graciously, Britain allowed the hapless French settlers to keep the land they had settled around Akaroa, on the condition they accept British citizenship, which they all did.

Avez-vous visité Akaroa?

Of course we visited Akaroa! Teresa and I hadn't been to our beloved Paris for several months, and we leapt at the chance to find just a little bit of France in the South Pacific. The drive from Christchurch, where we were staying, was a real rollercoaster ride. There's a death-defying "summit road" that careens along the ridge-top of the Banks Peninsula to Akaroa. It was every bit as harrowing as our drives through New Zealand's Southern Alps. Guardrails? Who needs them? Fortunately for us, there was no one else on the road that day, but for a few *blasé* sheep, to hear Teresa screaming from the passenger seat as we slithered around each hairpin turn.

Elle a gardé son caractère Français?

Yes, we were delighted to see how much French character the village still possessed. There were bistros and brasseries, French flags hanging in the windows. The street signs were "*rue* this," and "*rue* that." The oldest buildings had a feeling that was quite familiar; we couldn't place it at first as French, but in the little town museum, we discovered these were built in the same fashion as 1800s houses in New Orleans, a city we know well. New Orleans was a French colony when Akaroa was first settled.

In the museum, however, we also learned that the *Frenchness* of Akaroa had dwindled to next to nothing during the first half of the twentieth century, as newcomers moved in and fewer French families remained. Then, in the 1960s, the village made the deliberate choice to start marketing its French heritage as a unique tourist asset. Old streets were renamed and reposted with their original "rue," and an annual French festival was organized that runs to this day. There is even an association of the descendants of the 33 original settler families who arrived on the *Comte de Paris* that keeps French cultural heritage alive on the peninsula.

Left: From the Akaroa Museum, an early settler wearing a traditional Basque cap. Right: Tim poses for his portrait by a statue of a French painter in Akaroa. Is this what they mean by life imitating art?

Ce qui a laissé une impression durable?

Ah, there was one sad story that seemed to me quintessentially French: the tale of Pompey the penguin. In 1904, fisherman Louis Vangioni discovered a yellow-crested penguin washed up and starving on a remote beach near Akaroa. Louis took him home and fed the "miserable" creature, gradually nursing him back to health on a diet of mussels. Louis named the bird "Pompey." A female of his species had recently been found dead on a beach nearby — apparently his mate. For weeks Pompey would swim far out in the direction where the dead female was discovered; yellow-crested penguins mate for life, and the villagers believed Pompey was bereft; he was searching for her, but in vain.

Louis writes that Pompey was thin and melancholy for a long time. But gradually he settled into life in Akaroa. Louis set up an open barrel for Pompey, lined with straw, in which he made his home. He became a regular figure in town: each day he waddled along the streets of Akaroa to go out to sea on his fishing trips, and then came home in the evening. By this time, Akaroa had become a tourist destination, and this tame and charming little penguin became a major attraction. Louis sent to England for specially made fine tea-sets, stamped with Pompey's image; they sold in the little town like hot cakes.

Pompey survived until 1917, when he was killed by boys (or perhaps dogs?) on a beach near Christchurch. The poor little penguin was so used to people being friendly towards him, he must have been caught unaware by this sudden savagery. But indeed, it would have been most peculiar for a community to have befriended a penguin at the turn of the century, when there was no notion of conservation or kindness towards wild creatures. I can only suppose these descendants of the French were swept up in the tragic romance of the heartbroken little creature, bereft and searching for his lifelong mate.

How very French.

Chapter 29

Kaikōura: Whale-Killing/Whale-Watching Capital of New Zealand

Teresa, ahead of me, grasped the bow railing with both hands as the captain suddenly throttled us forward through the choppy blue waves. I hung on to the deck railing just behind my beloved. How I admired her adventurous spirit, braced like the brave heroine from *Titanic*, her chestnut hair streaming behind her in the wind.

The captain was chasing a whale. More specifically, two humpback whales that the crew had just spotted, barely 20 minutes into our whale-watching cruise off the coast of Kaikōura. Our hefty catamaran zoomed over the waves, turbo powered for speed — but also because turbo jets are significantly quieter than propellers, which can interfere with whales' echolocation.

Two spouts blew just off the starboard bow, and the captain killed the engines. We let go of our grips and strained our eyes, watching for the next spout. I stepped up beside my beloved.

"You looked so adventuresome just then, at the bow," I said in her ear.

Teresa turned and looked at me like I was crazy.

"I was *terrified*," she blurted out. "I was *paralyzed*. I couldn't let go or I knew I would fly over the rail! I was sure this time for sure, *this* is how I *die*."

The ship rocked up and down as we bobbed and drifted in the waves. Teresa had taken seasickness medicine on the advice of the cruise company before we departed. Now she looked a little unsteady. The humpbacks spouted and we could see their great black backs, no more than 30 meters (100 feet) away. The two were traveling side by side across the bay.

Kaikōura, 180 kilometers (112 miles) north of Christchurch, bills itself as the "Whale-Watching Capital of New Zealand," and for good reason. There are whales here year round, as well as many more that migrate along the coast and often stop for some leisurely feeding. Less than a kilometer offshore, there's a deep underwater canyon. Nutrients well up from the depths, providing an abundance of krill for baleen whales like the humpbacks, and deeper down, the larger delicacies preferred by sperm whales: giant squid, sharks, and other deep-sea fish.

The humpbacks spouted again, even closer to us this time. In the aftermath of the spray, a pungent odor wafted over the deck, like a cross between old garbage and an old fart. The captain's voice spoke over the loudspeaker: "If you smell something kind of funky just now, that's the whale's *breath* you are inhaling."

Who knew? Whales have halitosis.

"Whale breath: this will be our new insult," I said to Teresa.

She smiled wanly. "I think I'm going to head to the back of the boat," she said. "I don't feel so good…"

"Seasick?"

"Uh huh," Teresa nodded, and made her way, a little wobbly, to the aft of the ship.

The captain had told us at the beginning of the cruise that if anyone felt seasick they should go to the rear deck, which was steadier in the waves than the bow. I watched Teresa go, knowing she would prefer to be alone while she regained her composure, then I turned my attention back to the search for the next spout, and then the next. From time to time, the captain hit the engines, so we would not lose the whales, yet not come so close as to get in their way. Her voice crackled from the loudspeakers again.

"Everyone, a crew member just told me the whales have gone underneath the boat, and are now on the opposite side…"

We all rushed to the port side in time to see the spouts heading away from us. I decided to go find Teresa on the aft deck. It was a shame she'd given up on the whales, but I understood: seasickness.

"The whales, they came right up next to me, then went right under the boat!" Teresa said when I reached her. "They were so close, I could have reached down and touched them. I saw the deep lines in the skin around their heads."

"What?"

"Then they dove right under the boat. There was only me and one crew member back here. When he saw the whales he yelled 'Holy fuck!' So I guess it's not usual to see them so close? Then he called the captain on his walkie-talkie. He seemed pretty excited."

"You are mighty intrepid!" I said to my beloved, with just a twinge of envy for her close encounter.

"I'm just glad they didn't *breathe* on me. I would have lost my lunch."

After the humpbacks moseyed along, the next hour of the cruise was pretty uneventful. Pods of dusky dolphins zoomed around the boat from time to time. They circled around us, and arced up into the air, as if they were as curious to look at us as we were to look at them. A fur seal swam past — there's a massive colony on the rocks at the end of Kaikōura Peninsula, several hundred of them, all drawn by the plentiful fish and octopus (see page C23). They loll about the shore, no longer afraid of people. A hundred and fifty years ago, humans nearly drove them to extinction in the quest for their lovely brown fur. Once, there were an estimated 2 million of them in New Zealand. Today, there are about 200,000. So, almost a century after seal hunting ceased, their numbers have recovered to only 10% of what they once were.

Near the end of our cruise, we finally located the grand prize of the trip: an adult male sperm whale. Some 60 or so of these behemoths are semi-resident near Kaikōura. The big boys hunt and feed deep down in the canyon for as long as 90 minutes, then they return to the surface to breathe for ten minutes or so, refreshing their blood vessels with plenty of oxygen for the next dive. We floated at an amiable distance away, and watched our whale breathe and spout.

Above the surface we could see his massive forehead, back to the blowhole, which is only one-third of his body length. Just his head looked like a floating giant redwood tree trunk. Eventually he dove, arcing his tail slowly up, up, into the sky, and then plunging into the deep. The crew was able to identify him by the unique notches on his tail as Mati Mati. They posted his vital stats on the video screen, as if he were a New Zealand rugby player.

Mati Mati dives deep

From the numbers, we could tell that Mati Mati was about the size of a train box-car. He would have been a prize catch when Kaikōura was the whale-*hunting* capital of New Zealand.

Whaling got its start in Kaikōura in 1842, when Scotsman Robert Fyffe set up the first of five whaling stations on the end of the peninsula. His crews didn't need large seafaring boats, because the whales fed so close to shore. When someone spotted a whale, the crews set out in rowboats, harpooned their victims, and dragged them back to the shallow rocky shores, where they were dismembered and their blubber melted down into oil. The whole end of the peninsula once reeked with the gruesome smell of it. The extracted oil was loaded into barrels, and then shipped off to England to light the lamps of the cities and grease the wheels of the Industrial Revolution.

Whaling, a grim and bloody business. Left: My photo of whaling plaques on the peninsula walk. Right: The teeth of sperm whales that have been scrivened into works of art by whalers (from the Fyffe House Museum's collection)

It's hard to imagine such a grim, bloody business as murdering a whale, let alone that three nations we consider socially advanced still kill on a commercial basis: Norway, Iceland, and Japan. In fact in 2023 Iceland lifted its temporary ban on killing fin whales — an endangered species, and the second-largest whale in the world.

The original building that Robert Fyffe constructed for this wretched operation still stands on the end of the peninsula. It's now a museum, which I visited the day after our cruise. Fyffe's business is what first brought Europeans to this area, though he also employed 70 or so Māori from the local tribes. Southern right whales were their main target. This species got its name because it was the "right whale" for whalers to hunt. The species is slow in the water, and renders a lot of oil compared to other whales, as well as baleen — the whalebone used to make women's corsets throughout the Victorian era.

Fyffe's success proved surprisingly fleeting, however, as the number of whales dwindled rapidly. In 1866, the *Marlborough Express* reported that "whales seemed to have abandoned coming to Kaikoura." The local economy crashed.

Well, what a surprise. Do you suppose the whales spread the word among themselves that Kaikōura was no longer safe? A fascinating study based on nineteenth-century whalers' logs from around the world revealed that "sperm whales were at first easy to catch — but almost immediately, the whales learned how to evade hunters and whaling success plummeted by 60 percent." The study hypothesizes that the whales passed information to one another through echolocation to avoid being slaughtered by the men in boats.

In the twentieth century, motorized boats and harpooning extended the reach and deadliness of the hunt. Since the southern right and other baleen whales were largely gone from Kaikōura, the focus turned to sperm whales. These were prized for the massive quantities of concentrated sperm oil stored in their heads. This horrific industry continued to operate right up until 1963–64, when the last local operation killed 248 sperm whales in just one year, before it went out of business.

In the decades that followed, the whales have returned, and this has given Kaikōura a second chance, too. But this time, as conservers, not killers, of the great whales. In 1987 five local Maōri families mortgaged their houses as collateral for loans in order to launch a whale-watching business. The first tours were offered in July 1989. Because of their strong, spiritually-based respect for all life, the Maōri owners set out from the start to make sure their business would respect both the whales and the marine environment.

By 2006, Whale Watch Kaikōura was attracting a million tourists a year, creating local jobs and bringing in an estimated 28 million NZ dollars in annual revenue. Despite setbacks — an earthquake closed the roads for a year in 2006, and Covid shut down the whole country in 2020 — whale watching, and the whole town that now depends on it, is thriving. Several other wildlife tour businesses have also started in the area (such as kayaking and bird photography), piggybacking on the draw of the whale tours.

There's an important lesson here that I touched upon briefly in the glow-worm chapter. Modern capitalism has been based on extraction — whaling, mining, industrial agriculture that kills the land with pesticides and artificial fertilizers. Extractive booms are inevitably followed by busts when the resource runs out or the market gets saturated. Maximizing short-term profit before the bust is baked into the model. Yet somehow the bust always comes as a surprise — an unforeseen disaster. This has been New Zealand's economic history in a nutshell. On a global scale, this model is leading our planet to ecosystem collapse.

What I think is remarkable is that New Zealand might be at a turning point. The New Zealand government seems intent on changing its economic operating system away from extractive capitalism and towards *regenerative economics*: where strength comes from resilient ecosystems; where nature itself is the valuable "product" that is maximized. The key, of course, in New Zealand, is tourism.

Whale watching, for example, depends not only on the presence of whales, but also on not damaging the surrounding ecosystem. Importantly, it depends on not over-exploiting the "resource." In Kaikōura there are strict limits on how many boats can approach the whales, how close they can get, and what technology they can use. For example, using turbo jets instead of propellers, and not using sonar to track the whales.

Whereas extractive capitalism produces "negative externalities" — code for bad side-effects, such as pollution — regenerative economics creates *positive* externalities. In the case of whales, when they dive deep in the trenches, they bring back to the surface with them swirling masses of nutrients that plankton feed on, enhancing the food chain. During their lives, whales accumulate tons of carbon in their massive bodies, and when they die, it all goes with them to the ocean floor, locked out of the atmosphere for centuries: 33 tons of carbon for each great whale, according to a study by the International Monetary Fund, which has proposed whale conservation as part of the solution for climate change. A whale is literally a carbon sink.

Teresa wanders beneath the worn whalebone arches in a Kaikōura memorial garden.

I remember, on our whale-watching cruise, leaning over the rails, observing Mati Mati floating at rest, simply breathing. I thought: Sperm whales live a long time. If Mati Mati were my age, 65, he would have lived through the last killing season in Kaikōura of 1963–64. Sperm whales also have the largest brain in the animal kingdom, five times the size of ours. We understand very little about how their minds work, but suppose, just suppose, that the older whales *remember* what we did to them and their families. Do we owe them, perhaps, a little more today than simply not murdering them? Do we owe them, perhaps, space to restore their numbers in an ocean free of pollution, nets, and propellers; space to carry on with their task of enriching the ocean food chain and sequestering massive amounts of carbon?

I believe we do.

Chapter 30

River of Wine: Marlborough

In our ten weeks in New Zealand so far, Teresa and I had stayed in chic hotels and cheap motels, beachside cottages and mountainside chalets, swanky downtown apartments, and even a former bank vault. But the one place we had not yet stayed was in the middle of a vineyard. As we completed our circuit of the whole South Island, we decided to make our last stay in Marlborough, the nation's most famous wine-growing region, world-renowned for crisp and flavorful Sauvignon Blanc white wines. So, when Teresa found a vineyard that rented out its *entire* tasting room as a short-term rental in the off season, we jumped on it.

As we drove from Kaikōura up the rugged mountain coast, we were sad to say goodbye to the Pacific Ocean, which we would not see again on this trip. Entering the wide and flat Wairau Valley at the heart of Marlborough, and then driving through the main town of Blenheim was frankly kind of a downer. It looked like the dullest town in New Zealand. The center had all the character of a strip mall, with a few pretty gardens. Rows of *pansies*? That's what they plant in a land so lush? This must be *Bland*heim.

Just past Blenheim, however, we hit wine country. The entire broad valley was wall-to-wall grapevines, with dramatic craggy hills to the north and south of them. We drove for about 20 kilometers (12 miles), passing dozens of wineries on the roadside, before finding the sign to Misty Cove Wines. A gravel road led us through endless rows of vines to a slate-black building with a pool in front of it. There was no one there, just us, alone in the tasting room and the entire vineyard.

We have arrived in Marlborough country!

The sliding doors were unlocked, the keys just inside. The polished wooden floor was long enough for indoor bowling. There was a gas fireplace, a full kitchen with an island and six barstools, plus a TV lounge. A party of 30 people would not have felt cramped in this space. Our hosts had left us some breakfast goodies on the dining-room table, and *two* bottles from their winery. Teresa announced that she was never leaving the premises.

The only way to lure Teresa out of our glorious tasting room was to go visit the tasting room of *another* winery. Fromm Winery was just a few vineyards down the road, an easy hop. Teresa chose them from all the winemakers in Marlborough because they make a lot of wines other than Sauvignon Blanc. One can buy NZ Sauvignon Blanc everywhere in the world. Teresa wanted to know *what else* the region's vineyards could do.

Fromm also got our attention because they have the audacity to use cork to stopper their bottles, not the ubiquitous metal screw top. It's not that one can't cork a New Zealand wine, simply that most producers are so small, they sell out and hold back no bottles to mature later. Fromm practically dares its customers to take a bottle home and wait for it to peak! Just to drive the point home, their tasting room displays the owner's collection of over 100 different antique corkscrews.

We set ourselves up on the vineyard's terrace for the tasting, with an upturned barrel for a table. Across the parking lot we could see sheep eating the grass between the dormant vines. Clever, we thought. Sheep to mow, and also fertilize, the soil ("Does this vintage have notes of merino?").

The lovely woman who poured for our tasting was a local, and this was her first job at a winery. So she was rather flummoxed when we asked her a question — one that we had been pondering all morning long. In fact, realizing we did not know the answer made us feel downright ignorant: "Is white wine only made from white grapes, or can it be made from red grapes too?"

While our hostess could not answer, she had a lifeline: the winery's resident wine expert was on hand. He had just finished a tour of the vineyard with some customers, and was now chatting with them at another barrel-top. She brought him over to our table. Stephen was wiry, with silver hair and wire-rimmed glasses. He spoke with a passion about Marlborough wines that reminded me of Carl Sagan talking about the cosmos, as if wine was the absolutely most fascinating topic in the entire universe.

Stephen told us that the color of the grape is *not* what determines the color of the wine. He said, for example, that "Champagne is often made with a blend of Chardonnay (white grapes) and Pinot Noir (red grapes). It's the skins of the red grapes that give red wine its color. So, if you leave the skins in with the crushed grapes, you get red wine. Pink Champagne, for example, is made by leaving the skins of the crushed Pinot Noir grapes in with the juice for just a few hours."

Before he could leave us, I asked Stephen my real burning question: "Why is it that New Zealand Sauvignon Blanc wines are renowned throughout the world while New Zealand

Chardonnays, Bordeaux blends, Shiraz, and Pinot Noirs are equally excellent, but you can't get most of them outside the country?"

Stephen warmed to the topic.

"Yes, our other wines are also excellent! But why would you pay to import a New Zealand wine to the US or Europe when it's much the same as the good vintages those countries already make themselves? But Marlborough Sauvignon Blanc wines are both excellent *and* distinctly unique."

We nodded. We often drink it ourselves in the US, and heck, you can even buy Marlborough Sauvignon Blanc in wine stores in Paris!

"So, what makes them so distinctive?" I prompted.

"Most Sauvignon Blanc wines from other countries taste clean and crisp, but they don't have much flavor. Ours are full of flavor." (We could hear Stephen's voice swell with pride at this point.) "If you open a bottle of Marlborough Sauvignon Blanc on one side of the room, you can smell the aromas clear over on the other side. Usually, when you get intense flavors in a white wine, it's also sweet. But not wines from Marlborough! They are flavorful and also crisp, which is what makes them so unique, and so popular. You don't get this combination anywhere else in the world."

"And why not?" I hated to keep pestering Stephen, who was being so generous with his time and knowledge. But I couldn't stop myself.

Enthusiasm undimmed, he continued: "Sauvignon Blanc grapes in other countries must be harvested before they are ripe to keep them from getting too sweet. Once the grapes are fully ripe, they have too much sugar, and the wine loses acidity (which is what gives it crispness). But here" — he gestured with a swirl of his arm, taking in the whole valley — "we get the hot sun in the daytime, which the Sauvignon Blanc grape loves, but then, because of our extreme southerly climate, the summer nights get cold again. The grapes ripen in the day, building flavor and sugar, but then cool down at night, easing off the production of sugar. They can stay longer on the vine, and get more ripe, without gaining the same sugar content as grapes grown in other parts of the world. *And* we get full flavors while the wines retain their acidity. That's what makes Marlborough Sauvignon Blanc so unique."

Mic. Drop. Honestly, we felt like applauding Stephen for so clearly and succinctly explaining the mystery to us.

Left: Dormant vines in wintertime remind me of Christ, crucified: his blood transubstantiates into wine. Right: Local brands of Sauvignon Blanc at the grocery store.

Our final day in Marlborough, I was able to hike into the forested mountains to the south of the Wairau River, and from that vantage, I could see the length of the lower Wairau Valley floor, covered with dormant vineyards, which from the distance resembled the fine brown fuzz on the surface of a kiwifruit, some whole hundred kilometers of it.

I could only imagine what this great valley must be like at harvest time, bursting with billions of ripe grapes under the warm, fall sunshine, a veritable river of wine. Not a river that flows to the sea, but rather a river of carefully harvested golden globules, crushed, fermented, bottled, and then shipped out to the port, and from there to flow across the world, ultimately splashing into wine glasses everywhere.

Marlborough's River of Wine, the Wairau Valley

Here's a quick sum-up of what we've learned about New Zealand wines from our various investigations:

- *Waiheke Island* (in the North Island): Bordeaux blends are their specialty. These are the wines that put New Zealand on the international wine map. Some of the island's prize winners have tied with the best vintages in France and California; it's easy to taste why. Because of the small size of most of the wineries, it's hard to find Waiheke wines outside New Zealand. Only a small number of Michelin-star restaurants have them on their menus. In New Zealand, though, the wines are not too expensive, and it's well worth a day trip to Waiheke to sample them.
- *Hawke's Bay* (east part of the North Island): This is perfect wine country for Shiraz and Chardonnay — those full-bodied, big-personality wines. You can find Hawke's Bay Shiraz internationally. But if you ever find one of their Chardonnays, please give it a try. It's nothing like the oaky California Chardonnays.
- *Otago Valley* (southern part of the South Island): This is the furthest-south wine-growing region in the world. The cool, dry climate, plus the mineral-rich schist-and-clay

soils are a perfect place for finicky Pinot Noir grapes. I find most of them have a distinctive, earthy aroma. Some call it the "forest floor." It's actually a bit sewer-like to me. But hold your nose if you have to, because the flavors are worth it — far richer and darker than Pinot Noirs from the northern hemisphere. Their Pinot Gris is also worth trying — dry and crisp, with a strong personality.

- *Marlborough* (north in the South Island): *Sauvignon Blanc!* But if you run across anything else from this marvelous, magnificent valley of vineyards, don't hesitate to unscrew and sip. If it's a bottle from Fromm, remember you will need a corkscrew.

Part Three

North Island Revisited

Chapter 31

How Mount Taranaki Became a "Legal Person"

Mount Taranaki dominates the southwest coast of the North Island like Mount Fuji dominates Tokyo Bay. Its near-perfect snow cone is stunningly beautiful. It was wreathed in cloud when we first saw it from afar on our drive into the Taranaki district on September 1, 2023, while traveling from the South Island back to Auckland. Teresa had booked us for three days into a B&B as close to the mountain as possible, with a full view of the shrouded peak from our backyard. Though not part of the typical tourist route, for me this mountain was an essential destination. Though only 2500 meters (8000 feet) high, Taranaki was surrounded by lush rainforest and laced with hiking trails.

Throughout that first afternoon, Teresa and I watched Taranaki play with that cloud-shroud as if it was a veil: one minute revealing a hint of a cone, a few minutes later completely concealing itself. Then, just before sunset, the mountain whisked its white garment away altogether, as if to say to all mortals in the land below, "*Ta da!* Here I am, glorious Taranaki!"

Little did we realize how propitious that magnificent self-unveiling actually was. On that day, September 1, 2023, at the conclusion of extensive negotiations with the Māori tribes of Taranaki, the Government of New Zealand officially recognized Mount Taranaki and the surrounding parkland as a legal person. Henceforward, the mountain effectively "owns" itself — or should I say, *himself*?

To the Māori, there is not the same division as in our world between human and nonhuman; their world is fully alive in a way ours is not. Major features of the land, such as mountains, are therefore anthropomorphized in myths into beings with their own stories, their own all-too-human emotions. In the case of Mount Taranaki, his myth is one of jealousy, humiliation, and love.

Mount Taranaki drops the veil (from our B&B's backyard).

Taranaki once lived next to four other volcanic mountains in the center of the North Island, south of Lake Taupō: Tūrangi, Ruapehu, Tongariro, and Pihanga. Taranaki was in love with Pihanga, but so was Tongariro, who was stronger. They fought over Pihanga, but Taranaki lost. Scarred and humiliated, he was exiled to the west coast. As Taranaki withdrew, his pathway carved out the long Whanganui River valley that runs from the interior to the Tasman Sea. When he arrived at the shoreline, he glimpsed the small but beautiful Mount Pouākai. He was drawn towards her, and loved her. Pouākai and Taranaki's children became the trees, plants, birds, rocks, and rivers that flow from their conjoined slopes.

Pākehā New Zealanders, however, had a different narrative. To the descendants of colonialists, the mountain was named

"Mount Egmont" in 1770 by Captain James Cook as he sailed along the coast, in honor of the first admiral of the British Navy, Lord Egmont. Egmont was then an old man, and likely died before he learned someone had named a mountain after him on the opposite side of the globe. In 2018, the name was officially changed to "Taranaki" on maps and government documents as part of the ongoing treaty negotiations with the Māori tribes of Taranaki, though until September 1, 2023, the national park was still named "Egmont."

The name-change is just one part of a major victory for the tribes who have patiently negotiated with the government for years over the confiscation of their lands during the "Taranaki Wars" of the 1860s and 1870s. This was a time when violence erupted between Māori and Pākehā after land was taken from the Taranaki tribes without being properly sold. Here's how Radio New Zealand reported the story:

> The deed recognised the Crown had breached [the terms] of the Treaty of Waitangi in relation to Taranaki Maunga [Mountain] including by confiscating almost half a million hectares (1.2 million acres) of Taranaki lands. The national park that contains Taranaki Maunga and surrounding peaks, which is currently called Egmont National Park, will be renamed Te Papa-Kura-o-Taranaki, which means 'the highly regarded and treasured lands of Taranaki'.
>
> The park and its contents will be vested as a legal person, named 'Te Kāhui Tupua' — so the park will effectively own itself. But its interests will be represented by Te Tōpuni Kōkōrangi, a collection of both iwi (tribe) and Crown appointees.
>
> — Radio New Zealand, "Taranaki iwi sign settlement: maunga, and park to be recognised as a person," September 1, 2023

I went for a hike up to the snowline of Mount Taranaki the following day. The mountain's vegetation at high elevation is composed of dense, low trees and bushes. The air was filled with birdsong. At one point, I paused to listen to a dozen or more tūi birds, each one riffing its own unique, improvised-jazz-like melody, as if played on a set of bells. Stoat traps were laid out here and there along the pathways, with signs warning hikers not to disturb the traps, as the stoats were killers of kiwis. There are kiwis on Mount Taranaki? Yes! In fact, they even live in the farm zones as far down as our B&B. Teresa and I could hear them in the evening, screaming their terrifying love calls from the wooded banks of a nearby stream.

At the snowline I found a T-bar ski lift. Much to my surprise, it was operating. Dozens of people were skiing and sledding in the warm, spring-like weather. I hiked past the lift, along a trail that was muddy in the sun, and covered with ice and snow in the shade. It made for treacherous trekking, as the path was steep and narrow, and as slippery as a ski-run. I was glad I had brought my hiking poles, and punched my way along slowly, thankful I was in no rush to be anywhere other than right where I was. Far to the east I could see the distant white peaks of Tūrangi, Ruapehu, Tongariro, in the very center of the North Island — Taranaki's estranged brothers.

I asked four hikers I met on the trail, who were locals, if they knew about the name-change and the new ruling on Taranaki, and they all did. My sense was that though they all seemed vaguely positive about it, the change was not all that relevant to their lives.

The hostess of our B&B, however, had a different opinion. Her family and her husband's family have been dairy farmers in Taranaki for generations. She told me they can tell which farms have been "handed back" to the local iwi, because on that side of the fence, the land is neglected, going to ruin. I volunteered that if it was tribal land to begin with it, isn't it their business what to do with the land?

She countered that what worried her about the current government's policies was "reverse racism." Māori were getting priority medical treatment — say someone needed a transplant, why should they be first in line? And preferential placements in university — even if they were only one-tenth Māori. After all, if they were all New Zealanders, shouldn't they all be treated equally?

This was a delicate moment between her and me. After all, Teresa and I were guests in her country and in her home. Neither of us wanted to be confrontational, and frankly, I was glad she had expressed her real thoughts to me so plainly. However much I disagreed, I had to step carefully.

I gathered my thoughts, then replied: "Ah, *reverse racism* — I hear a *lot* about that in the US. I keep in mind the point that African Americans have explained to me about this: Racism is a *system* where one group of people dominates another. It's different than a person being racist — which is an attitude. For example, while a black person can be *racist* against white people, so long as whites are dominant in the US, *racism* can't move in the opposite direction. Any parts of the system that seek to compensate for white dominance by giving black people more opportunities is not 'reverse racism.' It's just 'reversing racism' by creating more equality for the minority."

A silent awkwardness followed. I dove in again (sometimes just can't stop myself).

"I'm glad I've had the chance to read a lot about New Zealand history since I got here — about the Treaty of Waitangi, how it was violated by the government in the late 1800s, and the Māori were dispossessed of their land. I think it's amazing that in past 50 years, the nation wants to honor its promises, and to make it right…"

"You know, we were never taught any of this history in school," my hostess replied. "Not like these days. We didn't know the past. Can you imagine how strange it was for my mother, that her grandchildren were learning to do the *haka* in school? In the New Zealand she grew up in, that would have been unthinkable."

Unthinkable. What an amazing word. These days, returning stolen lands has become *thinkable* in New Zealand, as has recognizing an indigenous culture's metaphysical view of a mountain as a spiritual entity akin to a person. It has become thinkable in New Zealand to allow more than one way of thinking.

I wondered if this kind of legal 'vesting' of a mountain with personhood is the first of its kind? How cool if it were to become a precedent in other countries as well — a new way of legally defining our relationship with our mountains, rivers, wetlands, forests?

With a bit of digging I discovered Taranaki is actually the *third* such designation of a geographic entity as a legal person in New Zealand. The first was Te Urewera, a vast forest in the northeast of the North Island, which was granted status as a legal person when the Tūhoe iwi settled with the Crown in 2014, and the former national park was turned back over to the tribe. Then in 2017, parliament passed the Whanganui River Claims Settlement Bill, giving the Whanganui River status as a legal person.

Just one week after the Whanganui designation, a court in northern India gave the Ganges and Yamuna rivers the status of "living human entities," citing the Whanganui ruling, and saying this would help in the "preservation and conservation" of these highly polluted rivers. What impact such court rulings will actually have is hard to say. If polluting these rivers now violates their "human rights," how do we stop it? Does a river have a right to flow freely — never to be dammed? The courts in India and New Zealand have yet to test them.

Meanwhile, the whole Taranaki community is on a fascinating journey. Their district website lays out a detailed roadmap for a "just transition to a low-emissions future" by 2050. It's an ongoing process of collaboration and vision creation that specifically acknowledges the role of the mountain as *Maunga*.

From the www.taranaki.info website:

Today we're leading the drive towards a prosperous and sustainable future with fresh thinking and an innovative spirit. Vibrant and stunningly beautiful, our ancestral Maunga guides and protects us, stretching to the Tasman Sea and an endless horizon. A horizon we're looking beyond.

While any attempt to chart a course to a desired future is bound to be fraught in an era of climate change, the very mountain that provides the region with its blessings also poses its greatest threat. Because Taranaki is *not* a dormant volcano.

Taranaki is the volcano "most at risk" of large eruption in the next 50 years in New Zealand, according to volcano researchers. The mountain first erupted a mere 130,000 years ago, and has erupted and collapsed many times since. Scientists have determined that on average it has a major eruption every 300 years, and it has been about 250 since the most recent one. So, *geologically*, this mountain's story is not one of jealousy and romance, but of destruction and rebirth.

Somehow, I do not think the Māori have a problem reconciling this volatile geology with their romantic mythology. For several hundred years, since arriving on these islands from Polynesia, they have endured and recovered from eruptions, earthquakes, floods, and other natural disasters — not to mention the conflicts with British settlers and the loss of their land. But they are a patient and resilient people. They survive. They rebuild.

Sketch of a thriving Māori village at Mount Taranaki in the 1860s (my photo from the Waitangi Museum). Local tribes flourished on the rich soil, adopting European agricultural techniques and trading with new settler communities such as New Plymouth. The settlers relied upon Māori produce for their survival, but became envious of their wealth. Hence, the Taranaki Wars.

Chapter 32

Auckland All Over Again

How the heck did we ever get back to Auckland? Oh, sure, you could say it was a five-hour drive from Taranaki, that's how we got here. But that's not what I mean. I mean, how did three months pass during which we drove from the north end of New Zealand to the south and back again in a long, lazy, figure-eight loop — and now our trip is over? It is as if we have been traveling through the country forever, and yet simultaneously as if it has been but a blink of an eye. How can slow travel seem to slip through our fingers so quickly?

Oh, don't cry for me, New Zealand! Teresa and I have had the time of our lives. We have always dreamed of visiting this remote, wild land, just to roam carefree beneath the wide southern sky. For Teresa, it has been thrilling to get *two* winters in a single year. She loves the cold, and loathes the heat. So being snowed in at Aoraki/Mount Cook in August was a peak experience for her. I got to climb volcanoes and spend days hiking in subtropical rainforests. Lost in a New Zealand jungle? That's my happy place. We looked out over Auckland harbor on our last day and agreed: we would do the entire journey all over again, exactly as we have done it. Only even slower next time. Three months was not really enough. I wish we could turn our figure-eight trip into an infinite möbius strip, looping round again and again like an amusement-park ride that never ends.

Returning to Auckland, I feel that I am seeing the city with a different set of eyes. As a metropolis of 1.5 million people containing fully one-third of the country's population, it seems like it could be anywhere in the Anglosphere — Australia, Canada, the Northwest United States. It's as if the city is trying hard to be generic, with the same architecture, international brands, marinas...

But now that I have been up and down and back again, I see some things differently here in the city known as "the Big Smoke." For one thing, our hotel, the Grand Hyatt, right by the marina, has spectacular Māori artwork mounted on its walls: paintings, tapestries, carved woodwork like the ornate paddle at the hotel entrance (below) commissioned from a master carver. But while these works of art are gorgeous, I remember learning that for the Māori, each motif, each character from their mythology, contains a special meaning that can't be separated from its location and its context. One can't simply extract the decor; the art is intrinsically part of a pattern woven into the identity of a time, a place, a people. And so to see such creations displayed on a hotel wall seems jarring to my eyes now.

At the Grand Hyatt entrance, Māori art, stripped of its significance. How could this carving possibly be merely decorative?

I had one last afternoon to hike through the city as an aimless flâneur, following my nose, opening my eyes to see what I might not have noticed at the beginning of my travels. In three months of wandering, I feel as if I have begun to tune in to what goes on beneath the surface in this brave new land, this Aotearoa/New Zealand: to read the signs that others might miss.

Not far from the Hyatt, the roof of some commercial enterprise — a store or office, I couldn't tell — was topped by a large neon sign that read: "WHATEVER" — the indifference of the modern city so literally writ large. I could not help but contrast that with the comforting neon sign on the top of the Christchurch Art Museum that beamed to its citizens the message, "Everything is going to be alright."

I also noticed in the crowded streets not one, but two Māori with *mōko* on their faces: one man and one woman, not together but in two very separate places. I've seen very few people wearing traditional facial tattoos on my travels, and remember seeing none at all from my previous eight days in Auckland. At a Māori cultural evening in Rotorua, it was explained to us that after falling out of fashion for several decades (it used to be hard to get a job if you had facial tattoos), mōko are being worn again by some Māori as an expression of their cultural identity. So I have to ask myself, had Māori wearing mōko been there all along on the streets of Auckland, but I simply failed to notice them?

Walking along one downtown road, I passed a threesome going the other way, and heard one woman say to her companions in a tone of matter-of-fact commentary, "American."

I was wearing a baseball cap, New Zealand T-shirt, and sunglasses. I had to own it. I hollered over my shoulder, "Right you are! I'm American!"

To my surprise, they hollered back at me: "Hey, American! Can we ask you something?"

I turned around and walked back to meet them. The three 30-something Kiwis explained they were a team in an "Amazing Race"-type competition, and on their list of tasks was to thumb-wrestle a stranger. Was I game?

Absolutely *yes!*

I pause here a minute for readers who might consider this a wrong answer. First: isn't this dangerous in a big city? Answer: no, not in New Zealand. It's perfectly safe. Second: what kind of crazy person would agree to thumb-wrestle a stranger in public? Answer: me. I've done improv acting for years, and the first principle is, say *yes.* Third: weren't you afraid of losing? Answer: oh, not at all. I'm fiendishly good at thumb-wrestling.

One of the two women of the Amazing Race trio stepped forward. She looked to be of Chinese heritage, though her accent was perfect Kiwi. She had long dark hair, and wore a bright, bubble-gum pink jacket. She held out her hand and gripped mine, thumbs up. One of her comrades raised his smartphone.

"Don't worry, I'll let you win," she whispered. "It doesn't matter. We just need to film it."

"Oh, you have to promise you won't 'let' me win!" said the American tourist. "I am very, very good at this! One-two-three-four, I declare a thumb war!"

The battle was on. To an observer across the street, it might have appeared there was some intergenerational jitterbug dancing taking place. A couple, hand in hand, were wriggling about, dipping and coiling apart and together, their arms writhing up and down, thumbs darting at each other like two fighting cobras.

She, too, was very good. Her thumb was very fast, very strong. She knew the moves. But I was wily. I slipped out of her holds again and again, and when she tried to get behind my thumb, I raised my wrist and turned, as if we were doing a swing-dance twirl. Hands high in the air, now upside down, I pinned her *digitus primus manus,* one, two, three. Her team cheered. They got the video! My defeated opponent, unabashed, gave me a quick hug and thanked me for being crazy enough to help them win their race.

I walked on alone, and soon came upon another message. Well, a literal and literary *set* of messages written in large white text on a big black wall. These were poems by a group of men and women, part of a diverse voices project, Phantom Poetry on Posters, sponsored by the international group Phantom Billstickers. I stopped to read them all, noticing that every other passing pedestrian just walked on past the wall, not even looking at it.

Two poems, both by Māori women, particularly spoke to me (below). "Shift" is about the connection between a person and her land in an age of ecological and spiritual violation. "Room" is an artful critique of patriarchy, reframing what it means to assume you are at the "center of the room."

Yes, signs are everywhere today, I thought to myself. Even this generic city can't hide the tectonic social forces pressing up, creating cracks, and then filling those cracks with new voices.

Before long I found myself in the main public plaza of the Central Business District, Aotea Square, flanked by the Auckland Council building on one side, municipal government offices on the other; there was a park on the third, and the Aotea theater and convention center on the fourth side.

There was a crowd at the convention center, with huge banners announcing the theme of the weekend event: Focus Forward. Wow, I thought — this *is* a sign! Was it a convention of futurists, or some gathering of social scientists, diversity experts, and youth representatives? Perhaps it was a weekend of community reflection in the final months before a pivotal national election? The doors were wide open, so I strolled inside for a gander (self-conscious that I looked exactly like an American tourist). No one noticed me. Everyone wearing a name tag was engaged in rapt conversation with their fellow attendees. The buzz in the room was electric. I found a program and discovered this was a convention of… real-estate property developers.

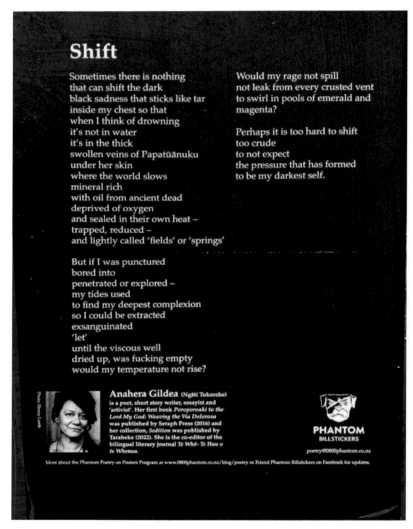

Shift

Sometimes there is nothing
that can shift the dark
black sadness that sticks like tar
inside my chest so that
when I think of drowning
it's not in water
it's in the thick
swollen veins of Papatūānuku
under her skin
where the world slows
mineral rich
with oil from ancient dead
deprived of oxygen
and sealed in their own heat –
trapped, reduced –
and lightly called 'fields' or 'springs'

But if I was punctured
bored into
penetrated or explored –
my tides used
to find my deepest complexion
so I could be extracted
exsanguinated
'let'
until the viscous well
dried up, was fucking empty
would my temperature not rise?

Would my rage not spill
not leak from every crusted vent
to swirl in pools of emerald and
magenta?

Perhaps it is too hard to shift
too crude
to not expect
the pressure that has formed
to be my darkest self.

Anahera Gildea (Ngāti Tukorehe) is a poet, short story writer, essayist and 'artivist'. Her first book *Poroporoaki to the Lord My God: Weaving the Via Dolorosa* was published by Seraph Press (2016) and her collection, *Sedition* was published by Taraheke (2022). She is the co-editor of the bilingual literary journal *Te Whē- Te Hau o te Whenua*.

PHANTOM
BILLSTICKERS

poetry@0800phantom.co.nz

More about the Phantom Poetry on Posters Program at www.0800phantom.co.nz/blog/poetry or Friend Phantom Billstickers on Facebook for updates.

"Shift," by Anahera Gildea (reprinted with permission of Phantom Billstickers)

Room

there are captain cooks amongst us too – bullies,
throwing their weight around

they think they are the centre of the room but that's only because
they have never been anywhere but there
they have no idea about the edges or even how far the room extends
one day they will realise that we in the corners are really in other centres
they will realise there are no corners
no walls

is it a room? is it a room then, when there are no walls?

i used to want to tell them to move over because they take up all the room
but there's no room
there is no room

no walls, no room - just links and connections and space

you're not at the centre; there are no centres
you're just standing there
one node in a massive network
like the rest of us

Alice Te Punga Somerville (Te Āti Awa, Taranaki)
is a scholar, poet, irredentist and māmā who writes and teaches
at the intersections of literary studies, Indigenous studies and
Pacific studies. Her publications include *Once Were Pacific: Māori
Connections to Oceania* (Minnesota 2012), *250 Ways To Start an Essay
about Captain Cook* (BWB 2021) and *Always Italicise: how to write
while colonised* (AUP 2022).

PHANTOM
BILLSTICKERS

poetry@0800phantom.co.nz

More about the Phantom Poetry on Posters Program at www.0800phantom.co.nz/blog/poetry or Friend Phantom Billstickers on Facebook for updates.

"Room," by Alice Te Punga Somerville (reprinted with permission of Phantom Billstickers)

Back outside, somewhat bemused by my misplaced idealism, I noticed across the square a large, lopsided wooden gateway. It brought to my mind the many ceremonial wooden gateways I had seen at the entrances of Māori community halls or other special places — bridges, ports, landmarks. Indeed, the name of the artwork was *Waharoa*, "Gate," created by the Māori artist Selwyn Frederick Muru. But, while traditional Māori waharoa were symmetrical, carved with formal tribal motifs, and not usually painted, this one was lopsided and brightly colored. As I approached, I could see it was etched all over with traditional motifs and also crazy-playful birds, fish, and other sea creatures. I was utterly entranced (see page C24).

Carved into one side of the waharoa, in both the Māori language and English, is what I took at first to be a traditional Māori epigram, but it was actually signed by the famous contemporary Māori poet Hone Tuwhare, and composed in the form of a Japanese haiku. This, in so many ways, was the message I was searching for, the message for the Māori people and their allies in their struggle for the restoration of their land and rightful place as full partners in the nation, the message for all those working to rebalance two centuries of self-inflicted environmental carnage, the message for all New Zealanders with a vision to build a better future. It was a message of patience, a message of endurance, and a message of hope, honestly, for all of us:

> *stop*
> *your snivelling*
> *creek bed;*
> *come rain hail*
> *& flood-water*
> *laugh again*

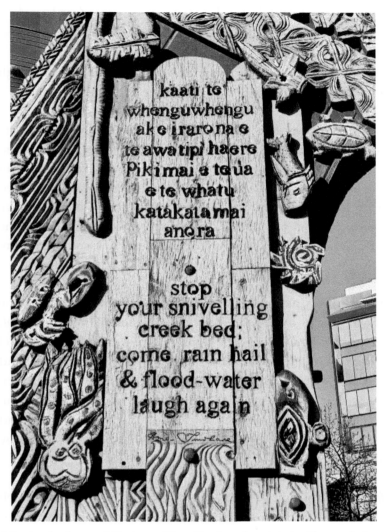

Haiku by the famous Māori poet Hone Tuwhare (reprinted with permission of Hone Tuwhare Charitable Trust) inscribed on *Waharoa,* "Gate," by the Māori artist Selwyn Frederick Muru

Advice for Slow Travel in New Zealand

For those who want to find their own path as flâneurs through New Zealand, here are a few travel tips:

Visas: If you want to come to New Zealand on a long-term visitor's visa, don't apply for the digital visa waiver program as we did — and regretted. It limits you to a maximum stay of 90 days. Instead, apply for a visitor's visa, which can be granted for up to nine months. If you are under 30 years old, and have a passport from a cooperating country, you can apply for the working holiday visa (for both options, see: www.immigration. govt.nz).

Hiking: If you plan on hiking/biking/mountaineering, it's fine to bring your own gear. But you absolutely must *clean all equipment before entering the country*. New Zealand has strict border controls to prevent the introduction of invasive pest and microbes, with thousand-dollar fines for attempting to bring in gear with mud or dirt on it. And they can refuse to admit you, too. Pack your bags so that you can easily access your gear and show it to the inspectors at the airport. This is no joke — they will check!

Off season: Travel in the cooler months (May–September), which is off season in most places except for skiers. It's much easier to book lodging in the off season, even though some hotels might be closed. In season, you must reserve well in advance, particularly for the main tourist destinations. Remember the North Island is warmer and more tropical than the South Island.

Weather: Prepare for rain. New Zealand is getting hit by more and more storms, some of which cause severe flooding. Bring the right rain gear when you hike, and (unlike me) obey all warning signs on and off the trail. It's also wise to build extra days into your itinerary to allow for bad weather. There were at least three destinations we hit where rain obscured the view for all but our final day at the site.

Sand flies: Traveling in the off season, we mostly avoided these tiny, biting pests. Even so, I would advise you to be prepared for them if hiking or beach-walking. Bring strong bug repellent and ideally a fine-mesh head-net. If camping, be sure you have a fine-mesh tent flap.

Driving: For long-term driving, check out monthly leasing options from various rental-car agencies, rather than renting by the day. We found it much more affordable. (See below for EV driving tips.)

Respect the kiwi! It should go without saying that you take care to obey all signs regarding wildlife protection for the kiwis and other endangered species on the islands. First and foremost, please don't bring a dog to New Zealand. They can't help but track and kill flightless native birds. Also, when driving, heed warning signs where kiwi, penguins, or other ground birds might be present.

Respect the Kiwi! Gosh, New Zealanders are nice. They avoid confrontation and do their best to treat each person with respect and natural friendliness. Oh, but it must get wearying in tourist season when there is an endless rush of demanding holidaymakers! So, please adopt their polite and patient attitude. Master these phrases: "No worries," "Sweet as," and if you must disagree, start with: "Yeah... Nah."

Driving an Electric Vehicle in New Zealand

We found it surprisingly easy to get around in an electric vehicle. It was also much cheaper than buying gasoline/petrol. If you, too, want to lighten your carbon footprint on the road, here are a few pointers:

Be sure you rent a vehicle with a long range (400km/230 miles) or more. Otherwise, on long drives you will find yourself making more than one charging stop a day.

If you are new to EV driving, insist the agency brief you thoroughly on how to drive and charge the car.

There are a few large charging networks in New Zealand that work with apps or fobs. The apps come with a map that shows all their charging locations in the country. ChargeNet is the main one, but more are coming online each year. Figure out what's best for you in advance.

It can take 30–60 minutes to recharge, so plan this around meal stops or food shopping (many charging stations are conveniently near stores).

In our experience, many Air B&Bs allow you to plug into their garage power outlets to home charge your vehicle. (We usually offered to leave some cash as payment.) To best take advantage of this, you should buy *an outdoor electric extension cord* that can connect your charging cable to the outlet, which might be some distance from where you park.

Never let your charge level get below 10% when driving. This brings on 'range anxiety' – the fear of running out of juice on the road. Usually, the navigation system in your EV will direct you to nearby charging stations, and some systems even warn you if you need a boost before reaching your intended destination.

Driving in cold weather will reduce the mileage in your battery, as does driving in excess of 50 miles per hour (80 km/h). You will find it easy to keep under this limit on all but a few major highways.

Remember an EV runs quietly compared to those noisy gas-guzzlers. Learn to honk *politely* to warn cyclists and pedestrians when you approach them on the road from behind. That goes for kiwis and penguins, too.

A note from the author:

I hope you enjoyed traveling with Teresa and me up and down New Zealand. If you want to join us on more adventures, please check out my travel blog: Medium.com/mature-flâneur. You can also read Volume One of our adventures: *Mature Flâneur: Slow Travel through Portugal, France, Italy and Norway*.

Tim Ward

**CHANGEMAKERS
BOOKS**

Transform your life, transform our world. Changemakers Books publishes books for people who seek to become positive, powerful agents of change. These books inform, inspire, and provide practical wisdom and skills to empower us to write the next chapter of humanity's future.

www.changemakers-books.com

Other Literary Travel Books by Tim Ward

Mature Flâneur: Slow Travel through Portugal, France, Italy and Norway

In the aftermath of the pandemic, author Tim Ward and his wife, Teresa, decided to leave their home and professional careers in the US to spend a year in Europe as flâneurs. The French word "flâneur" means one who "wanders without purpose, observing society." As the French literary critic Sainte-Beuve explained it, to flâne "is the very opposite of doing nothing." Indeed, it is to give yourself the gift of time: permission to live an unstructured life and, by so doing, discover something about the world, and about yourself.

Zombies on Kilimanjaro
A Father-Son Journey above the Clouds

On a journey to the roof of Africa, a father and son traverse the treacherous terrain of fatherhood, divorce, dark secrets and old grudges, and forge an authentic new relationship.

Savage Breast
One Man's Search for the Goddess

We think of God as male, but the most common representation of the divine through our history has been the Goddess. When did this major change happen, and why? Tim Ward went on an epic search through the ruins of ancient Europe to find the answers. What he discovered changed his life — and his relationship with women.

What the Buddha Never Taught
20th Anniversary Edition

A humorous behind-the-robes account of life in a Thai forest monastery. A cult classic.

Current Bestsellers from Changemakers Books

Resetting our Future: Am I Too Old to Save the Planet?
A Boomer's Guide to Climate Action
Lawrence MacDonald

Why American boomers are uniquely responsible for the climate crisis — and what to do about it.

Resetting our Future: Feeding Each Other
Shaping Change in Food Systems through Relationship
Michelle Auerbach and Nicole Civita

Our collective survival depends on making food systems more relational; this guidebook for shaping change in food systems offers a way to find both security and pleasure in a more connected, well-nourished life.

Resetting Our Future: Zero Waste Living, the 80/20 Way
The Busy Person's Guide to a Lighter Footprint
Stephanie J. Miller

Empowering the busy individual to do the easy things that have a real impact on the climate and waste crises.

The Way of the Rabbit
Mark Hawthorne

An immersion in the world of rabbits: their habitats, evolution and biology; their role in legend, literature, and popular culture; and their significance as household companions.

9781803417486